THE MENTAL HEALTH AND WELLBEING HANDBOOK FOR SCHOOLS

of related interest

Teen Mental Health in an Online World
Supporting Young People around their Use of Social
Media, Apps, Gaming, Texting and the Rest
Victoria Betton and James Woollard
ISBN 978 1 78592 468 2
eISBN 978 1 78450 852 4

How to Be a Peaceful School
Practical Ideas, Stories and Inspiration
Edited by Anna Lubelska
ISBN 978 1 78592 156 8
eISBN 978 1 78450 424 3

Can I Tell You About Compassion?
A Helpful Introduction for Everyone
Sue Webb
Illustrated by Rosy Salaman
ISBN 978 1 78592 466 8
eISBN 978 1 78450 848 7

Starving the Exam Stress Gremlin
A Cognitive Behavioural Therapy Workbook on
Managing Exam Stress for Young People
Kate Collins-Donnelly
ISBN 978 1 84905 698 4
eISBN 978 1 78450 214 0

The School of Wellbeing
12 Extraordinary Projects Promoting Children and
Young People's Mental Health and Happiness
Jenny Hulme
ISBN 978 1 78592 096 7
eISBN 978 1 78450 359 8

How to Create Kind Schools
12 Extraordinary Projects Making Schools Happier
and Helping Every Child Fit In
Jenny Hulme
ISBN 978 1 84905 591 8
eISBN 978 1 78450 157 0

The **MENTAL HEALTH** and **WELLBEING HANDBOOK** for Schools

Transforming Mental Health Support on a Budget

Clare Erasmus

Foreword by Chris Edwards

Jessica Kingsley *Publishers*
London and Philadelphia

First published in 2019
by Jessica Kingsley Publishers
73 Collier Street
London N1 9BE, UK
and
400 Market Street, Suite 400
Philadelphia, PA 19106, USA

www.jkp.com

Library of Congress Cataloging in Publication Data
A CIP catalog record for this book is available from the Library of Congress

British Library Cataloguing in Publication Data
A CIP catalogue record for this book is available from the British Library

ISBN 978 1 78592 481 1
eISBN 978 1 78450 869 2

Printed and bound in Great Britain

Contents

Foreword

By Chris Edwards

Back in the halcyon days of the English Language IGCSE days, when working as a deputy head and part-time English teacher, I used to have the dubious honour of being the assessor for the speaking and listening assessments for a cohort of 250 Year 11 students. This involved each being allocated a 10 minute slot, where they would talk for 3–4 minutes on a topic of their choice, whilst I hastily constructed a series of questions to occupy the final 6–7 minutes of our time together. As you'd expect, many students chose to talk about sport, a passion I share, which enabled me to sail through the Q&A with impressive panache. This wasn't the case with some of the outliers, however, whose chosen subjects included dragons, rollercoaster mechanics and Kim Kardashian, amongst other niche interests.

Concerningly though, the most striking aspect of this experience was the number of students who chose to talk about the pressures of being a teenager in this age of technology. I was absolutely aghast at the trepidation that these youngsters described in the build up to posting something as innocent as a photograph of themselves online. The number who spent hours using apps to modify their looks, terrified that someone would notice a blemish which could be mocked, was incredible. Many talked about the pressure to gain 'likes' to demonstrate popularity and the absolutely relentless, 24/7 urge to stay connected to social media for fear of missing out.

Shortly after the aforementioned assessment period came exam time. A young lady who I was mentoring absolutely flew through her English exam, which delighted me, but when it came to the time to go into her other exams, she froze, crippled with anxiety and couldn't step over the threshold into the exam hall. On speaking to her later, she explained that she had felt no fear in English as 60% of the final grade had already been acquired, but the linear exams, which would represent 100% of the fruits of 11 years of labor, were too much for her to bear.

I promised myself at that moment that I would do my utmost to prevent anything like that happening again. It really affected me, and I felt that I had let her down by not spotting the severity of her anxiety and putting things into place to help her. Furthermore, I felt angry that not enough had been done to prevent her reaching that level of angst, in the years building up to this terminal stage of compulsory school life.

Like many who were trained in my generation of teachers, mental wellbeing was never mentioned in our formative years in the profession, so I didn't know where to start. Needing a team around me to try to start building, I approached Clare, who jumped at the chance to grow such an important strategy. I also showed my commitment to the cause by marrying the daughter of Rita Rebholz, a wonderful lady who has a doctorate in adolescent mental wellbeing, which was a costly but vital development.

If you are starting this journey as a Head or senior leader, be aware that, as the modern saying goes, 'There will be haters.' I'd expect there to be a minority of people in any establishment who are blissfully unaware of Abraham Lincoln's 'Melancholy' or Winston Churchill's 'Black Dog', believing that anyone claiming any form or mental illness simply needs to 'man up' and stop being a 'snowflake.' In fact, one of my biggest regrets was not speaking up when a former leadership colleague derided a child for refusing to leave his bedroom for an exam due to his apparently crippling anxiety.

However, it is exceptionally rare to conceive a strategy where every member of staff is on board from the outset. Sometimes, as a leader, you need to accept that it may take a while for the 'laggards' to hop on board but be assured: they will. They will, because they will realise the urgency of giving some sort of support to our young people who need it so desperately. I was once told on Twitter by a teacher, hiding behind a pseudonym and a profile picture of a cartoon character (as so many seem to), that the idea that teachers should be involved in mental wellbeing provision is 'absurd'. Now, whatever your thoughts on the lack of external funding to support schools in this domain, refusing to engage in any sort of pre-emptive work to support your students' positive mental wellbeing seems quite contrary to the very reason most of us join the profession.

It is likely that fear plays a large part in the protests. But I have found that using Dr. Rebholz's analogy of a continuum from 0-10, (with 0 being perfect mental wellbeing and 10 being full mental breakdown) very useful in explaining that it is our job to keep students below a level 5, where we would expect the real experts to become involved. Nobody is saying that we are trained health professionals, but we do have a duty to guide students towards choices and behaviors which positively affect their mental or physical health.

What Clare is able to get across in this book, in her own inimitable style, is how to go about the daunting prospect of setting up a whole school strategy in this critical area. She will not claim to have resolved the world's problems in the field of youth mental health and wellbeing, but her pioneering work is inspirational, as well as being absolutely replicable. Every step of the journey is broken down in the finest of details and this book should be read by anyone who has responsibility for leading any sort of educational establishment. Together, we can create a real movement to benefit our youngsters and there can be no better place to start than the pages which follow these words.

Preface

This book was written in response to the multitude of emails and messages I received from teachers, teaching assistants, headteachers and parents seeking advice on how to support the mental wellbeing of young people in a school setting. What they all had in common was very little or no budget and a sense of feeling overwhelmed and not knowing where to start. I have written it as a user-friendly handbook to accompany any teacher or designated lead on mental wellbeing, with a micro budget, starting out on the road to support the mental wellbeing of their students.

When I started blogging three years ago, there were limited resources and not much advice for school teachers, but in the space of three years an incredible wealth of information has become available. I have written candidly of my own imposter syndrome and hope that my anecdotes and approaches will help build the confidence of the teacher in realising they really are the best person to have that first conversation with a young person when the worrying signs are spotted.

The book was completed just after the UK Government released in July 2018 its *Government Response to the Consultation on 'Transforming Children and Young People's Mental Health Provision: A Green Paper' and Next Steps*.[1] On reading the

---

1 *Government Response to the Consultation on 'Transforming Children and Young People's Mental Health Provision: A Green Paper' and Next Steps* (2018) London: Department for Education.

consultation and the UK government's response, I found some key positive messages:

- The plan is to have a mental health lead in every school and college by 2025.

- Mental health support teams will be created, and trained staff will be linked to groups of schools and colleges. They will offer individual and group help to young people with mild to moderate mental health issues, including anxiety, low mood and behavioural difficulties.

- The UK Government wants to reduce the time it takes to get treatment from children and young people's mental health services.

- Further research will be conducted into how social media affects the health of children and young people.

- Further research will be conducted into how to ensure better support for families who need more help.

- Further research will be conducted into how to prevent mental health problems, bringing together different mental health experts.

However, I also had a number of problems with the proposals:

- The mental health lead is not mandatory.

- The training and financial provision for the mental health lead is still being developed. Who will train these teachers now, what will the training look like and who will pay for it?

- The mental health support teams still need to be trained, put together and the logistics sorted out. Will children in all schools in all areas be reached or only some?

- It is going to take some years to further research and report on findings on how mental health problems can be prevented. We need to change the narrative *now* to ensure that there is a lifestyle shift in our society so that we embrace a culture and environments that encourage positive mental wellbeing, resilience and holistic values.

- The Green Paper is still reactive and does not look at education policy and policy makers. It fails to pledge further research into the impact of a narrow curriculum and rigorous assessment and exam culture on children's mental health and wellbeing.

This book is perfectly timed to be the stepping stone before all these government measures come into force.

The UK Government talks about schools having a 'lead on mental health' but this immediately makes you think about what must be done for students struggling with mental illness. Although this would be part of their brief, schools need to be doing so much more to develop a culture that fosters wellbeing for everyone. Wellbeing is a much more inclusive word that embraces the diversity of need – and that includes the wellbeing of teachers. It also acknowledges that all dimensions of development and experience contribute to a young person's ability to flourish and learn.

Dr Sue Roffey wisely states: 'Wellbeing is a not a panacea but a framework that fosters optimal outcomes for everyone and a supportive environment when challenges occur.'[2] This handbook is for all current and future mental wellbeing leads and education practitioners who are wanting to make a start in developing a robust proactive and pre-emptive mental wellbeing framework that 'fosters optimal outcomes for everyone'.

The series of chapters cover five key aspects, giving readers step-by-step strategies for working within the current constraints of school systems:

---

2   Roffey, S. (2019) *The Primary Behaviour Cookbook: Strategies at your Fingertips.* London: Routledge, p.1.

- The school in providing curriculum time and space to talk about mental wellbeing and to develop a culture in promoting positive mental wellbeing.

- The individual students' level of engagement and seeing relevance to take part.

- The role of the staff and their own mental wellbeing.

- The role of the parents in engaging in mental wellbeing conversations and promoting lifestyle choices that encourage positive mental wellbeing.

- The extent to which the local community gets involved, and engaging the services of local external agencies.

If we get this right, we could help build a society where mental wellbeing is a universal priority and regarded with equal importance as physical health.

If we get this right, all staff would be trained in how to spot the signs and what language to use in holding that first conversation about a young person's mental wellbeing.

If we get this right, *all* schools could have a robust and effective staff referral system for these young people which would ensure there is someone in the school concerned specifically with such matters.

Our role is not to diagnose or to replace child and adolscent mental health services (CAMHS) but if we are proactive and pre-emptive with the language we use and the emotional literacy we teach our students, we could help stop a situation from escalating.

If we want to be truly pre-emptive, it is important we change the language of learning with all teachers, parents and students, emphasising the following:

- Our mental wellbeing is linked to our academic results and we need to ensure that as a society we don't neglect the first in pursuing the second.

- Failure can be seen as a route to success. It's what we learn from our failures that is important.

- Self-worth and success are not dictated by academic results.

- The whole person has value, not just how they perform in exams.

- Mental wellbeing issues arising in school can follow a student into adult life.

Finally, I have written this book based on more than 20 years' teaching experience and being one of the countries earliest heads of whole-school mental wellbeing. Everything I know I have collaborated on and read and gleaned off others, so my sincere thanks go to: Dr Rita Rebholz, Dr Pooky Knightsmith, Mike Armiger, Teresa Day, Charlie Waller Memorial Trust, Nina Jackson, Natasha Devon, Chris Edwards, Leah Stewart, Dr Emma Kell, John Shepherd from The Resilience Doughnut, Dr Tim Obrien, Viv Grant, Dr Sue Roffey, Professor Jonathan Glazzard, Caro Fenice, Hannah Wilson, Sue Cowley, Bukky Yusuf, Patrick Ottley-O'Connor, Roy Souter, Shirley Drummond, Sue Webb, Alison Kriel, Lynn McCann, Annie Poole, Vivienne Porritt, Jaz Ampaw-Farr, James Hilton, Tim Smith, Dr Kathy Janzan, Nicola Lainsbury, East to West, Cathy Jones, Natalie Spencer, Kathryn Joyes, Kay LeMarquand, Charlotte Watkins, Julia Davies, The Carnegie Centre of Excellence for Mental Health in Schools, The Magna Carta School, Brighton Hill Community School and, of course, my incredibly patient publishers Jessica Kingsley.

1

Make a Start

KEY POINTS

* Don't double up the roles of lead on mental wellbeing and the special educational needs coordinator or pastoral manager. Keep them separate.

* Look out for who is already championing mental wellbeing support for students and staff in your school.

* Note that the UK Government wants every school and college to have a designated lead in mental health by 2025.

Do not try to replace the specialisms of a mental wellbeing nurse or psychiatrist

I need to start at the very beginning and be honest about my qualifications. Yes, I do have a degree – a Diploma in Higher Education and an Honours degree – but it is not in psychology or counselling or social work or mental health. My experience for this job came from the fact that I have over 20 years' teaching experience of working with teens and am passionate about equality and inclusion. Back in 2011, I helped my students produce a groundbreaking anti-homophobia film called *Homophobia – our closeted education*[1] and launch a whole-school anti-homophobia awareness campaign which eventually

---

1   https://vimeo.com/128591375.

resulted in us speaking at national teaching conferences and secondary schools up and down the country. This quickly led to a massive grassroots anti-bullying campaign and working with fabulous external agencies like The Diana Award,[2] and implementing the student anti-bullying ambassadors programme. I became a key contact in the school for the lesbian, gay, bisexual and trans (LGBT) awareness campaigns and anti-homophobia campaigns, and I was the anti-bullying coordinator. Without realising it, I had already started on a key strand of delivering vital mental wellbeing support.

When you look for your designated lead on mental wellbeing, it is often the person who has already started championing aspects of this pastoral work in your school. They won't take much convincing. They are already halfway down the road. Giving them this management title will be sending a clear message to your entire school community that you are taking this area of young people's education very seriously. Ensuring it is an experienced member of staff who works closely with the senior leadership team will give it the gravitas it deserves if you want all staff, students and parents to take it seriously.

This way you can really start to open the discussions about what mental wellbeing is and promote the vital campaigns that it is okay to talk, there is no shame, we all have mental health. This has been widely advertised under the hashtag #Timetotalk.

When I was approached with the opportunity of becoming the lead on mental wellbeing I initially jumped at the opportunity, then a shadow of doubt came over me as I asked myself, 'What qualifications do I have?'

Often this is the first mistake that schools can make. Of course, teachers are not able to replace the work of mental health professionals in treating or diagnosing mental health conditions. Thinking in this way is bound to stall the process of supporting adolescent wellbeing in your school as you are not able to offer this support. Schools do need to realise that

2   https://diana-award.org.uk.

the mental wellbeing work that they can be involved in is pre-emptive. Using Dr Rebholz's scale where perfect mental wellbeing is a 0 and a mental breakdown is a 10, schools can play a vital role in keeping students below a 5.

We should aim to set up an environment which encourages the development and support of the 'whole child'. We are involved in a crucial stage of youth development where, together with the family, we can be pre-emptive and proactive and help prevent the escalation of mental wellbeing challenges that may then need intervention from an already overloaded CAMHS.

Once you have got your lead on mental wellbeing, you need a team of adult wellbeing mentors. These are your frontline staff who will be working with the students on a one-to-one basis, or in groups. This is where you spend some essential money on training such as the Mental Health First Aid (MHFA) course or those currently being offered for a lead on mental health and wellbeing by the Carnegie Centre of Excellence for Mental Health in Schools, part of Leeds Beckett University. Look for the staff who already have mentor qualifications and experience and are already keen to attend levels 1 and 2 of the counselling course. Try and appoint staff in their sole capacity as adult wellbeing student mentors.

Separate special educational needs and mental wellbeing areas

One of the mistakes a school can make is to appoint an adult wellbeing student mentor who then has to double-up as a special educational needs coordinator (SENCO)/pastoral manager/ teaching assistant. Keep special educational needs (SEN) support, pastoral behaviour support and mental wellbeing support separate. Let students know that learning needs and mental wellbeing needs, although often linked, are essentially different. Have different spaces and different staff allocated.

Many of our older students have appreciated this because when they wanted to talk about something personal they did not want to go to the SEN centre because they did not have a learning need. This hampered the process of students seeking help and support.

When a student with concerns is referred via a staff referral system, the young person's present state should be quickly triaged, looking at data on attendance, behaviour, attitude to learning, and home life. It is at this point that a decision should be made to either arrange a pastoral behaviour-centred intervention, an SEN intervention or a mental wellbeing intervention.

Start now. Appoint a senior member of your staff as the lead on mental wellbeing. Place mental wellbeing objectives in your school development plan with a focus for both staff and students starting with conducting research into listening to what they have to say about the mental wellbeing barometer and needs for your school. It is important you do this now because it has been pledged in the UK government's *Transforming Children and Young People's Mental Health Provision: A Green Paper.* Here it stated:

> We want every school and college to have a designated lead in mental health by 2025. The designated lead will be a trained member of staff who is responsible for the school's approach to mental health.
>
> This designated lead will:
>
> - oversee the help the school gives to pupils with mental health problems
>
> - help staff to spot pupils who show signs of mental health problems
>
> - offer advice to staff about mental health
>
> - refer children to specialist services if they need to.

Every school and college need to make sure that the structures and the roles are in place so that the 'designated lead in mental health' can embed these priorities.

2

Listen to and Identify the Wellbeing Barometer of your School

Dr Rita Rebholz and Clare Erasmus

KEY POINTS

* Listen to your students and staff before rolling out initiatives.

* Do some research using focus groups and specially crafted and considered questionnaires.

* Take time to understand the school situation, audit what you already have in place and do a 'stress test' to see what you can realistically deliver.

The purpose of a mental wellbeing programme in a school should be to destigmatise, raise awareness and promote positive lifestyle choices for mental and emotional wellbeing. But often it is difficult to know where to begin. The demographic nature of each school and community will be different and so will their related needs. The mental wellbeing barometer will differ too.

I often get asked: Where I should start? What should I do? My automatic reply is that your mandate has to come from the student and staff voice. It is essential that schools *listen* to the needs *before* they roll out whole-school initiatives. What might make sense and be right for a small school in rural Surrey won't be necessarily relevant for a large inner-city school in Hampshire. Doing your research does take time but it will be worth it in the end because your data will drive your initiatives. Missing out this step will mean you are not identifying needs specific to your school community, and therefore you are not ensuring that the initiatives are grassroots-led and relevant.

When I was working in a large comprehensive school in Surrey, our student voice was ascertained through a comprehensive research project entitled 'A model of excellence to promote student mental wellbeing within the secondary school environment', led by researcher Dr Rita Rebholz. Rita stated:

> It is our aim to provide a health-promoting environment in which students can thrive academically and emotionally. To this end, we place emphasis on ascertaining 'the student voice' to ensure the strategies/services we provide to support those with mental wellbeing difficulties are commensurate with students' expressed needs.

We used a flexible, multi-method case study, which was underpinned by the significant theory of salutogenesis[1] and the concept of social capital[2] to elicit 'the student voice' on matters appertaining to students' mental health and wellbeing while in the secondary school environment. Data collection methods were derived from both the qualitative (focus groups) and quantitative (questionnaire) traditions.

---

1   An approach focusing on factors that support human health and wellbeing, rather than on factors that cause disease.

2   The networks of relationships among people who live and work in a particular society, enabling that society to function effectively.

The two datasets were then analysed according to a facilitative and complementary approach[3] and in keeping with the assumptions of the paradigms from which they originated. The qualitative data was analysed manually within a framework of five steps,[4] involving data reduction, data display and conclusion drawing. The quantitative data was analysed using Survey Monkey (due to availability at the school), and the use of a quota sample of 204 students enabled cross-tabulation of the data to yield insightful findings from the perspective of year groups and gender.

The project took approximately one academic year to complete and involved one hour focus groups with four year groups and a quota sample of students who completed the student mental health and wellbeing questionnaire online.

The focus group sample involved approximately 5 per cent of the school's cohort. Students were selected from Years 7, 8, 9 and 10, with an even representation of gender, SEN needs and those qualifying for 'pupil premium'.

The qualitative data was gathered from the focus group sessions in one day. The sessions were held in the headteacher's office to give the process gravitas and to help the young people who were invited to talk feel valued.

The focus group sessions were digitally recorded, and a member of staff made notes on a flip-chart, which were used to complement, support or challenge the verbatim transcriptions.

The questions posed in the focus groups were informed by the following considerations: social support networks, a sense of belonging within the school environment, social relationships, trust in others, tackling issues of inequality (such as discrimination and stigma) and mental wellbeing problems. The questions were also based on a school audit of existing

---

3   Brannen, J. (2004) 'Working Qualitatively and Quantitively.' In C. Seale, G. Gobo, J. Gubrium and D. Silverman. *Qualitative Research Practice*. London: Sage, pp.321–326.

4   Adapted from Miles, M. and Huberman, A. (1994) *Qualitative Data Analysis: An Expanded Source Book*. London: Sage.

support service provision which identified areas of strength and areas that could be further investigated.

Over 20 questions were asked. For example:

- What things make you feel happy?

- What things do you worry about?

- What things worry you most at school...and out of school?

- Who would you turn to at school if you were feeling worried or unhappy?

- Do you believe you would be supported/helped here at school with a problem you might have?

- Do you know what is available to you here at school to help with any problems you might have?

- Can you name any of these services?

These results then in turn informed the type of detailed questions we asked when collecting quantitative data in the questionnaires we conducted using Survey Monkey.

Based on the initial results, we were then able to make informed decisions about what *our* students needed. For example, across each year group the responses consistently revealed that students did not know:

- *where* to get support for mental wellbeing

- *who* to talk to

- *when* to go.

It was because of this overpowering data that we were clear about the need for the Wellbeing Zone. Data such as this can drive the initiatives in your school and ensure that you are targeting where the need is for your specific demographic.

We were also able to ascertain specific needs for each year group; for example, for our Year 7s: body image, puberty and coping with changing rooms in PE. In Year 8, the areas of need were all about belonging, identity, friendships, relationships and feeling valued. In Years 9, 10 and 11, it was consistently about coping with increasing workload, uncoordinated homework deadlines, exam pressure, extensive extra revision sessions and ultimately self-imposed pressures to meet the teacher's expectations and to get that much-desired target grade.

Finally, before you begin rolling out your whole-school mental wellbeing programme, it is also vital that you conduct a 'stress test' to assess what you currently have in place, the provisions you can put in place and what this allows you to offer in terms of support. Basically – what is your school's capacity for coping with the demands of offering support?

Note: I am very aware that not every designated lead will have access to doctoral level researchers, but it is worth contacting your closest university to see if there is a postgraduate student who would like to help you conduct your research. At the time of going to print, organisations that you could contact to help you with your research are:

- *Anna Freud National Centre for Children and Families* – offers schools a wellbeing measurement online survey and report enabling schools to understand areas of strength and the challenges facing their students by using a set of validated questionnaires that focus on emotional and behavioural difficulties, life satisfaction, resilience and support networks. A small fee is charged. See www.annafreud.org/what-we-do/schools-in-mind/our-work-with-schools/wellbeing-measurement-for-schools.

- *Education Support Partnership* – the UK's only charity providing mental health and wellbeing support services to all staff working in education. It provides schools and colleges with surveys to assess staff wellbeing and then helps with addressing any issues raised. See www.educationsupportpartnership.org.uk/staff-engagement-wellbeing.

3

Raise the Finance

* Invite the local press to document your initiatives – you will be surprised at the 'wellbeing warriors' in your local community who will then come forward to volunteer and help.

* Match projects to relevant local businesses. Find out what their altruistic focus is.

* Call on the parents in your school who have links with the local, county or national business community; they can be an invaluable network for contacting the right people.

News headlines such as 'All state schools in England "to face funding gap by 2020"' (BBC, 17 March 2017) and 'Education funding falls £400 million' (TES, 6 August 2018) have been haunting our media timelines. The reality is that subjects, staffing and resources are all experiencing a massive squeeze. However, while we protest and campaign for political parties to stick to their manifesto pledges, the education of our young people must go on.

It might be prudent at this point to reflect on the emphasis African cultures place on family and community and the relevance of this timeless Igbo and Yoruba proverb, 'It takes a village to raise a child'. While the squeeze takes place it is more

26

important than ever for UK communities to rally around their local schools and their local children. It is vital that parents, local councils, local businesses all come on board as a collective and help financially educate the children in their 'village'.

As teachers, managers and senior leaders we cannot expect people to simply 'gift' us money. We must be creative and bold, and pitch and ask for the funds we need. Securing funds from grants has become ever more vital and competitive. Here are some tips to start you off:

1. Break down all your projects into small amounts – anything from £100 to £30,000. Every amount matters.

2. Match projects to relevant local businesses. Find out what their altruistic focus is. Sometimes your school's project could be promoting just the type of public image the business would like to associate itself with. For example, one school obtained funding from its local Tesco Groundwork scheme for an outdoor sensory garden to support the mental wellbeing of SEN students and for an after-school outdoor learning centre focused on biodiversity and studying local ecosystems.

3. Contact parents in your school who have links with the local, county or national business community. They can be an invaluable network for contacting the right managers or even chief executive officers.

4. Look at all the council and county funding sites and read their guidelines carefully for eligibility criteria. Take note of what each funding pot is looking to award money for. Tailor-make your project to fit it. Take note of the deadlines.

5. Make contact with your local council and county health and wellbeing committee. Engage with representatives from these boards and work together with them when planning a whole-school campaign which may involve

the parents. They may have funding from the National Health Service (NHS) or CAMHS available to support your initiative.

6. Pitch. Albert Einstein is reported as saying: 'If you can't explain it, you don't understand it well enough.' Aim to sum it up in three lines and elaborate in no more than 300 words. State clearly the need, your vision and objectives, and the project and desired outcomes.

7. Make contact with your local further and higher education institutions. See if you can pilot projects where the college/university students get to do volunteer work with your students on mental wellbeing-related projects as part of their research and training and development.

8. Make contact with the local counselling course. All counsellors have to volunteer a certain amount of free time before they can qualify. This could prove to be very helpful for the one-to-one sessions with your individual students.

9. Track down your local Healthwatch[1]. This organisation is the independent national champion for people who use health and social care services and it is keen to get young people involved in being active and to speak up and help to make services better for their communities.

10. Tap into all free training and initiatives pledged by the UK government. For example, currently every secondary school is entitled to free mental health first-aid training from MHFA England.[2]

11. Invite your local Member of Parliament to visit your school, and obtain their support in enabling mental wellbeing and wellbeing initiatives to take place.

---

1   https://www.healthwatch.co.uk.
2   See www.gov.uk/government/news/secondary-school-staff-get-mental-health-first-aid-training.

12. Invite the local press to document your initiatives – you will be surprised at the 'wellbeing warriors' in your local community who will then come forward to volunteer and help. In my school, we had a mindfulness teacher come and deliver a series of mindfulness training sessions for our staff as part of our Health and Wellbeing Week.

13. Finally, be brave, bold, and relentless in your requests – our schools need the collective support from the extended community now more than ever.

14. Get yourself a Twitter handle and start following #mentalwellbeing ambassadors who are doing fantastic work in schools and the key #mentalhealth hashtags for organisations like YoungMinds, Heads Together, Time to Change and MHFA. You will see lots of free stuff offered, and campaigns you can join and benefit from.

4

Start at the Top

KEY POINTS

* You can't support student mental wellbeing without addressing the mental wellbeing of staff.

* The UK Government has produced a helpful *Workload reduction toolkit* that school leaders can use to help identify areas affecting staff wellbeing and actively aim to reduce teacher workload.

* Change the culture in our schools ensuring life–work balance and destigmatise the topic of mental health. Have spaces and people for staff to talk to.

Sick staff = absent staff = inconsistent teaching and learning

It would be remiss of any leadership team to think it was possible to tackle student mental wellbeing without simultaneously focusing on the needs of their staff.

In her book, *How to Survive in Teaching*, Dr Emma Kell cites alarming statistics about the teacher crisis:

> Some 42 per cent would disagree with the statement 'I am happy in my work' and 66 per cent have been tearful at work. Some 52 per cent would strongly disagree with the statement 'my workload is manageable'. I would argue it's not about the amount of work, but about the nature of the tasks.

Respondents told me the biggest contributor to the workload issue was: meetings that go on too long; duplicating data; not enough time to eat, hydrate and rest in the day; monitoring and checking up – questioning their professional integrity.[1]

The workload of teachers is a recognised national issue and if we are to improve the staff retention and recruitment crisis then engaging in this research will help you hear the different voices of your staff on issues of their mental wellbeing.

The UK Government has made great strides in showing its commitment to reducing teacher workload and produced a new paper that details what it is doing to reduce unnecessary workload for teachers. Published in July 2018, the *Workload reduction toolkit*[2] provides support for schools with a range of materials to help review and streamline workload through solution-focused and collaborative discussions. It offers three stages for schools to work through:

1. Identifying the workload issues in your school so that you know the areas to prioritise.

2. Considering the key themes causing teacher workload. There are suggestions for workshops, tips from leaders, and tools and case studies to help you make changes.

3. Evaluating the changes you made and measuring impact.

I highly recommend that the designated lead on mental wellbeing and the senior leadership team look at the resources provided, which include:

- Identifying the issues in your school – a workshop for staff to discuss survey findings.

- Example staff workload survey – to help identify workload issues.

---

1 Kell, E. (2018) *How to Survive in Teaching: Without Imploding, Exploding or Walking Away*. London: Bloomsbury Education, pp.4–5.

2 www.gov.uk/guidance/reducing-workload-in-your-school.

- Example structured conversation template – to gather feedback from staff.

- Impact graph workshop – for staff to identify the workload impact of tasks.

- Impact graph template.

It is essential that we not only tackle the workload issue, which is a huge contributor to reduced mental wellbeing, but also the culture of management in our schools and the related stigma attached to staff admitting that their own mental wellbeing is reaching a crisis point.

The Carnegie Centre of Excellence for Mental Health in Schools at Leeds Beckett University conducted a survey in December 2017 with more than 700 teachers. The data showed that that poor teacher mental wellbeing can have a detrimental effect on student mental wellbeing, student progress, the quality of teaching and the quality of the relationships that teachers establish with students and colleagues.

Professor Jonathan Glazzard, who led the research, wrote:

Teachers who completed the survey stated that poor teacher mental wellbeing can detrimentally affect:

- their ability to plan lessons

- their creativity

- the quality of their marking and feedback

- their behaviour management skills

- their ability to respond to the needs of learners, including those with mental wellbeing needs

- the progress of their pupils

- the quality of their explanations in class.[3]

---

3   Glazzard, J. (2018) 'How are you really doing?' *Teach Primary*, March, pp.64–65.

Colleagues often feel they can't say anything as it immediately results in them being micro-managed even more and could affect their career progression.

A middle manager in a school once told me that he had complained about coping with the workload and excessive staff absences in his department and the impact this had on him arranging cover, and he had felt that his mental wellbeing was at tipping point. The response from the school was that he should go and see his GP and get a mental health diagnosis. This made the colleague feel even more vulnerable. He just wanted someone to listen to him, recognise why he was feeling the way he was and hear his call for more support. The fact that nothing was in place in the school made the colleague feel as if he wanted to leave, and resulted in him taking considerable time off.

Trust is a key component in building a culture which prioritises wellbeing for all. It is important the research into your school's mental wellbeing in the workplace is led by a member of the senior leadership team and that they communicate the findings to the staff community and are actively seen to implement changes where appropriate. This process can be achieved by using Survey Monkey and allowing staff to respond anonymously. School leaders really need to allow staff to share their thoughts and feelings and it helps if there are sections for additional comments. It also helps if the leadership team can have some transparency with the staff, and the entire set of results, including comments, are published for all staff to review (some comments may be intensely personal and for the sake of protecting identity, it may be necessary to edit some of these).

The staff questionnaire should seek to ascertain staff mental wellbeing in the workplace (a generic example of this is provided in Appendix 3 at the back of the book and there is another one in the *Workload reduction toolkit* mentioned earlier). The leadership team should not assume they know what the results will be or be afraid of hearing the truth. I have heard of one school which simply did not want to follow through with the survey because they felt it would 'open up a can of worms'.

Ignoring the problem is the worst thing a school can do

Just engaging in the process of issuing the questionnaire shows that you are listening, and collecting the responses is part of the process of being prepared to provide an environment which prioritises support for staff mental wellbeing.

Ideally, this process would be repeated annually to monitor progress and to guide future policy making, ensuring that the environment supports staff mental wellbeing.

As a follow-up to the survey I would encourage staff to be invited to form a focus group to help analyse the results and feed back to the leadership team, coming up with action plans and strategies for change. This helps ensure that the collective staff voice is properly represented and it does not slip into the 'blaming game', with the leadership team accused of being selective about how they read into the results. Some call this group a *staff wellbeing action group*.

When analysing results, it is important that we are honest about what is achievable and what is personal responsibility. These are vital steps, showing you are engaging with your staff. I have seen schools show that they are listening to staff by preparing a 'You said. We did' response within the half term of finding out the results. Often it is just small 'quick wins' (like committing to meetings not going over schedule; feeding staff healthy food on parents' evenings; having cups in the staffroom and tea, coffee and milk; or cutting back on double-data entries and too many meetings), but a quick response is greatly valued.

However, sometimes the results will show that there is a culture of bullying from line managers; that staff are feeling micro-managed and over-observed; that their ability to take risks and have autonomy over their teaching has been removed and it is all prescriptive; that they are working incredibly long hours to keep up with the school feedback and assessment policy and providing evidence of progress; that they feel if they open up about their declining mental wellbeing it will affect opportunities of promotion and lead to further micro-management. These issues will indicate clearly that there needs to be a shift in the culture of the school and the entire management style, and teaching and learning expectations need to be balanced with staff wellbeing.

It's no surprise that in many schools, the major factor revealed about staff wellbeing is coping with stress. In Surrey, this resulted in a few schools holding whole-staff in-service training on mindfulness as a practice and rolling out an eight-week voluntary training programme using the .b Foundation mindfulness course from the Mindfulness in Schools Project.[4]

This sounds great for schools with the budget, but with current financial constraints this might be beyond many schools' financial capabilities. I have been in correspondence with a few headteachers on the initiatives they have tried. Here is an account of what headteacher Roy Souter at Stoke Hill Junior School in Exeter managed to do on no budget:

> In September 2016, we carried out our first staff wellbeing questionnaire. I wanted to find out how staff were feeling about their role, as well as identifying specific areas where changes to school policy could improve wellbeing.
>
> In terms of wellbeing, we found that our teachers felt well trained for their role, but that our school policies around assessment, marking and planning were more time consuming than they needed to be. The other key thing that had a negative impact on wellbeing was the lack of consultation before change – they weren't unhappy about the changes per se but felt that they didn't always know why the changes were being made and weren't consulted about the implementation process.
>
> So, to improve wellbeing, our focus has been on revising school policies to reduce the amount of time that our procedures take. For example, we no longer ask teachers to provide written feedback in maths books and have drastically reduced the amount required in English books. We changed our reports, which are now much shorter. We never give teachers tasks to complete after staff meetings, and we provide time to complete

---

4   https://mindfulnessinschools.org/teach-b-foundations.

required administrative tasks. All these changes were made following a real consultation process.

These changes cost us nothing, but the impact has been massive. Standards have been maintained – our teachers are professionals and make sure the children are given good quality personal feedback to help them improve. Teachers have time to develop their own interests outside school, and we have virtually no staff absence. Our follow-up survey shows a big increase in teachers saying that they are happy in their work, that they feel consulted about changes, and that their workload is manageable.

Schools need to recognise that staff who have mental wellbeing challenges should feel as supported as those with physical challenges. Unfortunately, there still exists the stigma that if they are not coping it is a weakness of the individual as opposed to looking at the system, the expectations and the workload. It is ironic that it is often middle leaders who crumble under pressure and when they cite their mental wellbeing as concerning the reply is often 'this is what comes with being a middle manager'.

There is a better way to respond. Senior leadership can pay more than lip service to making staff feel valued. They are a school's currency. Invest wisely in their wellbeing and you will reap the benefits. I have been lucky enough to interview some great headteachers who are role-modelling positive mental wellbeing values to their staff, in their opening address on the first day of in-service training. Here are some extracts they have kindly shared with me.

Shirley Drummond, Headteacher at St Helen's College, Hillingdon:

As we embark upon a new school year refreshed and energised, please can we keep our school motto (written by the children) at the core of what we are about:

- Strive for excellence

- Help others achieve

- Care for each other.

This motto is for the whole community – and without you all, St Helen's College would not be the place that it is. For us to give the pupils the experiences and education that we offer it is crucial that we look after ourselves and each other. Please maintain that work–life balance for your own mental wellbeing and wellbeing. We are so aware of looking after the needs of our pupils, but remember, if we are not at our best the children will not benefit.

Our mindfulness programme is in full swing for the pupils and parents again this year; I am very aware that staff have already participated in a full foundation course but if there are any new staff who would like the opportunity to participate in an eight-week course then do let me know and we will see if we can arrange it for this year.

We also have some surprise guests making an appearance in classrooms this year when our 'Worry Monsters' join the children. However, please can I urge everyone that if you do have a 'worry' of any sort – be it home or school – we are here to listen and support you all. Let's keep all our wellbeing intact. It is so important that we support each other to get the best from every single one of us.

Here's to another great year!

Chris Edwards, Headteacher at Brighton Hill Community School:

This year, I want to assure all my staff that I am prioritising your wellbeing. We will be running a number of initiatives, such as the secret buddy scheme, Biggest Loser, 'Golden Apple' award for staff member of the week, breakfast cooked by the senior leadership team and so on, but I have also brought in 'Dependent Days' whereby staff who have dependents are not penalised financially for missing school to support them. I want staff to know I fully support them if they have a crisis at home. In fact, I will go so far as to say that if I find out you are working with me while missing important family responsibilities, it will disappoint me greatly.

Hannah Wilson, Executive Headteacher of Aureus School and Aureus Primary School, is doing some groundbreaking work with her values-based school in Didcot, Oxfordshire:

> This year we will grow, learn and flourish as a team and as a community. We will strive to nurture the hearts and minds of the whole child. Our values will bring our vision to life in every decision and action we make.
>
> At Aureus, staff wellbeing will underpin student wellbeing. Our mindfulness programme, our family dining experience, our community reflection time, our personal development time and our gratitude practice will remind us why we teach. Every member of the Aureus team is a teacher, a team player and a role model. You are all leaders, you are all valued and you all have a voice. I am proud and privileged to be working with you.

I want to end this chapter with words from Patrick Ottley-O'Connor's in-service training day speech to his staff. Patrick is a leadership development coach for schools and multi-academy trusts and a visionary executive headteacher:

> Today, on our joint in-service training day, as Executive Principal with the Essa Foundation Academies Trust, I will repeat the message to all staff.
>
> Be the wellbeing change that you want to see and to be a mental wellbeing and wellbeing supermodel yourself.
>
> We will continue to place wellbeing at the heart of school improvement and ask ourselves 'How will this benefit the learners and how best can we support staff to make the difference?'
>
> We will continue with: Themed Acts of Kindness; Wellbeing Advent Calendar – daily wellbeing treats in December; Wellbeing Star of the Week – weekly nominations by staff for staff to recognise support for their mental wellbeing and wellbeing.
>
> It is essential to look after yourselves first, before helping others, so that together we can make a real difference for our learners.

Tips to improve staff mental wellbeing

- Mindfulness

- Quiet rooms

- Staff suggestion box

- Staff recognition board and nominating a colleague

- Coaching culture

- Providing cover so that staff do not miss key family events such as the nativity play, parents' evenings, school sports days

- Going home at 3pm once a week

- No emails after 6pm

- Wellbeing buddy schemes

- Free yoga classes

- Subsidised gym membership

- Biggest loser weight-loss competitions

- Senior leadership team cooks breakfast

- Flexi/job share schemes

- Phased-in maternity leave returners

- Links with nursery schools attached to the main school

- Tea and Talk mental wellbeing chat sessions

- Fewer meetings, with a capped length

- Revised assessment policies, with emphasis on feedback

- Clerical tasks reduced – reviewed every year

- Wellbeing staff action group to arrange events and advertising in staff areas.

5

What is Resilience?

KEY POINTS

* Set up a school environment where the concept of resilience is accurately explored and understood.

* Resilience is about looking at what's available to you – within yourself and within your environment.

* There are many factors which a young person has available to them, to help support and develop resilience.

Resilience isn't just about grit and not giving up. It's about recognising your strengths and recognising the support available to you.

Most schools have an excellent focus on teaching and learning and ensuring each child is tracked and makes academic progress, but it is just as vital that they also facilitate an environment that enables our young people to be more resilient and better equipped to meet life's challenges.

There is a real misunderstanding about resilience that it is just about 'not giving up'. Here is an analogy: if you were stuck in the snow without food and water – having resilience is not remaining passive and seeing how long you can endure the hell for. That would be a foolish decision and certainly lead to a painful death.

Resilience is about being an active participant, recognising your strengths and your positive relationships and knowing what resources and support are available to you to help you work through a challenging situation. So, using the 'stuck in the snow' analogy, it would be about recognising who is available to help you; how far you would have to go to get help; what you have in your toolkit to help you survive; what your options are for getting yourself out of danger and into safety. Resilience is about looking at what's available to you – within yourself and within your environment – to work through the challenge.

I have had the opportunity of working with John Shepperd from The Resilience Doughnut, and he talks about 'the process of resilience' and suggests that we need to focus on 'doing resilience', rather than 'being resilient'.

The Resilience Doughnut was developed by clinical psychologist Lyn Worsley at the Resilience Centre, Australia, as a simple yet practical resilience-building tool that can be easily used by anyone, including young people. The model is outlined in her book, *The Resilience Doughnut: The Secret of Strong Kids*. Since its development in 2008, The Resilience Doughnut has been research-validated, recognising a decade of positive impact.[1, 2]

1   Worsley, L. (2011) *The Resilience Doughnut: The Secret of Strong Kids.* Eastwood: Lyn Worsley Psychology Services.

2   Worsley, L. and Hjemdal, O. (2017) 'Scale Development and Psychometric Qualities of the Resilience Doughnut Tool: a valid, solution focused and ecological measure of resilience with Australian adolescents.' *Journal of Solution-Focused Brief Therapy*, 3.

According to John Shepperd, The Resilience Doughnut has two parts:

A. The hole in the middle represents the person's key beliefs that develop as they build the tools and resources they need to face the world.

B. The Doughnut is comprised of seven sections, each section representing an external factor in the person's life. When reviewing the research, Worsley found that these seven factors repeatedly showed up in the lives of resilient people:

1. *The Parent Factor* – characteristics of strong and effective parenting.

2. *The Skill Factor* – evidence of self-competence.

3. *The Family and Identity Factor* – where family identity and connectedness is evident.

4. *The Education Factor* – experience of connections and relationships during the learning process.

5. *The Peer Factor* – where social and moral development is enhanced through interactions with peers.

6. *The Community Factor* – where the morals and values of the local community are transferred, and the young person is supported.

7. *The Money Factor* – where the young person develops the ability to give as well as take from society through employment and purposeful spending.

These seven factors each have the potential to enhance the positive beliefs within the person and thus to help the individual to develop resilience.

You can find out more about The Resilience Doughnut at: www.resiliencedoughnutuk.com.

6

Train Staff

KEY POINTS

* Train all staff on the signs to look out for and how to hold that first conversation.

* Set up a culture in the school where mental health is everybody's business.

* Ensure that structures are in place for teacher/tutor interventions to take place and tracking of these interventions.

It is important that all staff are trained in 'how to spot the signs' for students who are struggling and in how to intervene early to help them build their resilience.

It is also important that all staff realise it is not about passing it on to someone else – we are all mental wellbeing gatekeepers, in a position to recognise a crisis and on the alert for warning signs, ready to share key information and hold that conversation. By training all staff you can stop the glut of referrals to one person and you can ensure that there is a culture of joint responsibility for supporting the mental wellbeing of all young people. All staff have a responsibility to monitor and support the young people.

It is vital that on the back of the student and staff questionnaire you hold whole-staff in-service training on the signs to look out for and how to hold that first conversation.

This includes teaching staff, support staff, catering, site and office staff. Anyone who has contact with the young people needs to be aware of the signs to look out for.

It is key that staff are encouraged to practise listening skills, asking the important questions and reinforcing the safeguarding lines which all staff are obliged to say:

> The only time I will break confidentiality and tell someone is if you give me permission by saying it is okay, or I think that you or someone else might be in danger of being hurt. In that case, I would need to tell someone to make sure that everyone is safe. I would talk to you about this before we as a school do anything.

In your training, you need to clearly point out some of the signs to look out for in the young person. These can be spotted in tutor time, class lessons, at break, lunchtimes and in extra-curricular activities. Here are a few:

- Erratic behaviour

- Erratic attendance and punctuality

- Changes in academic progress – losing interest, failing to hand in work or avoiding presentations

- Changes in attention and focus, becoming disruptive

- Mood swings and violent outbursts and helplessness

- Complaints of pain, nausea, headaches, needing the toilet a lot

- Becoming increasingly withdrawn and having crying spells

- Increasing low self-esteem and reluctance to be singled out

- Frequent self-criticism, self-blame, seeking constant reassurance

- Visibly anxious and agitated

- Considerable change in personality

- Physiological signs such as chronic fatigue or sleeping too little

- Changes in diet

- Appearing unkempt and neglected

- Engaging in risk-taking behaviours

- Reports of abuse from others or self-abuse

- Change in positive friendships circles and relationships with others

- Concerned reports from parents

- Safeguarding reports from police and social workers.

You need to point out that the first stage of support could be anyone from the classroom teacher, the tutor, the break-time duty staff member or the the sports coach. The big questions to ask yourself are:

- How much of an impact is this having on the young person's life?

- How long has it been going on for?

- Is this a trend? Are they coping? Are there others or is it just this child?

- How much of a change is there in eating or behaviour?

- What can be done?

We are not asking the schools to diagnose or to replace CAMHS, but what we should expect is that every adult in the school has the capacity to be a compassionate, caring, empathetic human being who will see it as their responsibility to listen. Our schools need to ensure we have adults who are trained to listen and spaces and time to hold that conversation.

Part of your in-service training for all staff should be to focus on *how* to hold that conversation. Here are some tips:

- It is essential that to begin with you go through key boundary issues and the confidentiality/safeguarding terms with them. In summary, this is that you cannot keep anything confidential if it is deemed that the child or any other person might be at risk of harm. You have a duty of care to report it. Be clear about who else will get to hear the report. It is vital that you are transparent otherwise you will lose their trust.

- Be clear about exactly how much time you have available (5/10/15/30 minutes) and set up a follow-up meeting to carry on the conversation.

- Make sure you find out why they want to talk to you.

- When listening, don't over react, stay calm. Give them your full attention.

- Listen without judgement and try to listen with empathy.

- It helps if you can paraphrase what they have told you to check for understanding and clarity.

- Sit with the silence.

- Try and ask questions such as: Who do you feel you can go to for support? Who do you have a good relationship with at home?

- Signpost where there is help in the school, at home and in the community.

- Research and share self-help strategies (*Gaia TeenMind* app is a great resource for this).

- Summarise – especially towards the end of the conversation – to make sure you and the student share the same understanding of what has been discussed.

- If you are signposting help in the school make sure you are clear about times , place and who will be there to chat to them. Keep this consistent and deliver on your pledge.

- Offer a plan of action, for example: another session to talk; a self-help strategy; a target to achieve this week; extra reading or audio-visual material to gain a better understanding of what is happening; agreed 'safe spaces' they could use at break and lunchtimes.

Do not:

- judge them and let them feel as if you disapprove, try to diagnose the problem and say 'it sounds like you have...'

- compare with your own story

- tell them it is something they must toughen up on and dismiss it as something they will get over

- promise anything by saying, 'leave it up to me' or 'don't worry, we can fix this for you'

- ask leading questions as this can compromise the facts later.

Unless it is a glaring safeguarding issue where the young person is at risk of harm or harming others, at this *first stage* your school could expect at least two weeks of intervention to take place with the young person and that adult. Ensure that you have a tracking system in your school to record this intervention. Many schools have software like SIMS where there is an intervention section, or Excel spreadsheets for each year group. Either way, it is important that this is recorded, and a conversation is had with the parents on resilience strategies they can come up with at home. If there are still no signs of improvement after two weeks, then you can refer it up to the adult wellbeing student mentor for additional one-to-one and group interventions.

The key to holding these conversations is that the young person feels safe, listened to and supported, enabling them to carry on attending school and stay focused on their learning.

Finally, I can hear my colleagues saying, 'So when do you expect me to do this? I have only enough time to prepare, assess and feed back. When do you expect me to hold "this" conversation?'

My reply is it needs to be the culture of the whole school and not down to just one teacher. This support needs to be factored in when drawing up tutor/pastoral directed time for every teacher. If the culture of the school is that it is everyone's business to support mental wellbeing, then this staggered way of giving support is more focused and coordinated, ensuring that it is happening in every tutor group. This way, it enables more consistent support which is hugely beneficial to students as they move up through the school; and we all know that early intervention is hugely beneficial not only to wellbeing but also to learning.

Note: For free training resources, if you visit the Charlie Waller Memorial Trust's YouTube site[1] there are some excellent PowerPoints and webinars delivered by Dr Pooky Knightsmith on handling disclosures and how to listen so that children feel heard and supported.

---

1   https://www.youtube.com/channel/UCPJauIgUy_B9N1BAI-N7A2Q.

7

Teach Students about Mental Health

KEY POINTS

* It is important to talk about mental health topics because it sends a clear message to the students that you recognise their importance and are prepared to have an open discussion.

* Mental resilience and wellbeing will form a key element of the new compulsory subject, health education.

* Before the lessons on mental health are taught, there are some key factors which *must* be in place to ensure safeguarding, safe exploration for discussions and follow-up.

It is vital to talk about mental health topics because it sends a clear message to students that you recognise their importance and are prepared to have an open discussion. By showing you have a clear understanding, they will feel safer with your confidence and the whole conversation can be destigmatised. One of the reasons why students don't approach staff or peers is because they feel people won't understand. Remember, the reason for delivering lessons around mental health is to support the students in developing their emotional literacy so that they are in a position to make an informed decision and keep themselves and their peers safe.

The UK Government has realised the value of each child developing emotional literacy about mental health, and learning to seek appropriate support as early as possible.

In the *Government Response to the Consultation on 'Transforming Children and Young People's Mental Health Provision: A Green Paper' and Next Steps* it was pledged that all schools would have to deliver health education as a compulsory part of the core curriculum:

> Mental resilience and wellbeing will form a key element of this new subject, as well as ensuring that pupils understand that good physical health contributes to good mental wellbeing.[1]

The objectives behind a scheme of work around mental health lessons are to ensure that the students are aware of:

- what it means to have good mental health and how lifestyle choices and decisions can influence our everyday mental health

- what the signs are of mental health illness and how to spot these signs

- where to go for help and how to signpost a friend when in school and out of school

- the fact that it is okay to not be okay but it's important we talk about it and reach out for support, and keep coming to school.

But before the lessons are taught there are some key aspects to consider:

- Does the classroom environment encourage safe exploration and discussions?

---

1   *Government Response to the Consultation on 'Transforming Children and Young People's Mental Health Provision: A Green Paper' and Next Steps* (2018) London: Department for Education, p.33.

- Is the teacher aware of safeguarding considerations and the need to look out for vulnerable students?

- Has the teacher read up on the lesson and any extra reading given and prepared for the range of questions they may get asked?

- Does the teacher feel confident about how to engage and steer classroom discussions, and what not to say?

8

Build Safe Classroom Environments

KEY POINTS

* Be familiar with the school's safeguarding policy and know what to do and who to refer to if a child makes a disclosure.

* Depersonalise the learning.

* Have an 'Ask-it Basket' for students to discreetly pop down questions for you to answer.

The following advice, much of which I have learned from the Charlie Waller Memorial Trust and Dr Pooky Knightsmith, is for any teacher delivering these classes.

- Ensure that the topics you are going to explore are shared with the lead on mental wellbeing, the mental health first aiders and the safeguarding team to see if any students in the class are flagged up as vulnerable students around the topics (if names are flagged up, seek advice from the practitioners who will know more about a student's personal and confidential case).

- Be familiar with the school's safeguarding policy and know what to do and who to refer to if a child makes a disclosure.

- Before you teach the lesson, familiarise yourself with material to see if any parts of it may be upsetting for your specific class cohort. Always plan the lesson with the most vulnerable student in mind.

- Give students a week's notice about what the next topic will be – this can enable students who have concerns or worries to approach you in advance about something they may feel uncomfortable with.

- Think about the possible questions you may get asked, the rumours or myths that young people may share and how you can keep the conversation moving forwards but at the same time allow for a safe and open discussion. Request from all students that they use their language carefully and don't reference any names, and ensure that ridicule and personal judgement have no place in the discussion. It may be useful to set up some ground rules in advance on how to listen and engage in a discussion which does not seek to hurt, condemn, undermine or humiliate others.

- Depersonalise the learning by using scenarios and case studies. Try and avoid using the personal pronouns 'I' and 'you'. Distancing the topic from the personal enables greater objectivity.

- Ensure that students are left with clear information about the definition of the topic – it is important you dispel any myths and rumours. Ensure that they are clear about the signs to look out for and where people can go for help in school and out of school, and what websites, helplines and reading material or podcasts and films they can turn to for additional support.

- Have an 'Ask-it Basket' (an empty basket in the room) for students to discreetly pop down questions for you to answer. These can be written anonymously, or the student could flag up their name.

- At the end of each lesson, show these words or have the 'Ask-it Basket' as a permanent fixture in your classroom and regularly draw attention to it. The information is clearly directing them to where and when they can get help in the tutor group and school. For example, in one school in Hampshire they have a #wellbeing square and in another school they have a Wellbeing Zone. Be clear with your signposting.

Do you have any questions from this lesson? Too shy to put up your hand? Then why don't you write it down and place it in your teacher's 'Ask-it Basket' and we can respond by covering the topic in a general discussion? Or you can talk to your teacher privately about it. Remember, if you feel you need to talk you have many routes available to you in the school – friends, teacher or wellbeing and antibullying ambassadors in the #wellbeingsquare.

9

Plan Mental Health Lessons

KEY POINTS

* Visit these websites for excellent lesson plans ready to adapt or roll out: Heads Together; PSHE Association; Time to Change; BACP; Samaritans; Cornwall Healthy Schools.

* Ensure that you read and make sure you are familiar with the school's safeguarding policy and procedures for managing disclosures.

* Gaia Technologies offers excellent mental wellbeing apps for both primary (Gaia Young Mind app) and secondary schools (Gaia TeenMind app). You can purchase the app as a single user or you can adapt and buy specifically for your school by visiting this link https://www.computingframework.co.uk/product/secondary-gaia-teen-mind

Writing mental health lessons from scratch can take time as they do need to be well researched and double checked for accuracy and safeguarding. Below are some excellent sources where you can find ready-made, validated lesson plans. All teachers will be used to adapting their material to suit the type of students in their class based on ability, level, personal experiences, and trust in the classroom.

Some superb mental health lesson plans

Organisation: Heads Together

Source: www.mentallyhealthyschools.org.uk/teaching-resources/lesson-plans-and-pshe-resources

Target: Early years foundation; Key stages 1, 2 and 3

What: A range of lesson plans, assembly plans and whole-school initiatives:

- *Spread a little kindness* – six short classroom activities focused on developing empathy and kindness.

- *Online safety* – lesson plans and classroom guidance about staying safe online.

- *Respect* – a selection of ideas and activities which focus on enhancing children's respect for themselves, friends, families as well as people in their local and wider community.

- *Differences* – classroom activities celebrating difference, diverse skills and teamwork.

- *Drinkaware* – these lessons cover topics on the law on alcohol; health and social harms associated with drinking alcohol underage; the effect alcohol can have on emotional health and wellbeing; the relationship between peer pressure and underage drinking.

- *Care and share* – designed to help children cultivate positive friendships and reduce the risk of bullying.

- *A Stonewall pack* – with a video exploring difference, diversity, identity, stereotypes, friendship and families.

- *Disrespect Nobody* – the Disrespect Nobody campaign is aimed at encouraging young people to understand what a healthy relationship is; to rethink their views of controlling behaviour, violence, abuse, sexual abuse and what consent means within their relationships; and direct them to places for help and advice.

Organisation: PSHE

Source: www.pshe-association.org.uk/system/files/Primary%20 lesson%20plans_0.pdf

Target: Key stages 1, 2

What: Primary resources:

- *Recognising feelings: identifying feelings words* – aims to give pupils a vocabulary for talking about and identifying feelings and emotions.

- *Recognising feelings words, 'big feelings' and expressions* – helps pupils to recognise a range of feelings in other people and to identify who and how to ask for help with some of their feelings.

- *Recognising feelings: hearing, drawing and being* – the focus is for pupils to build on the range of feelings they can identify in themselves and in others. Pupils are given opportunities to practise strategies for ensuring someone listens to them when they need to talk about how they are feeling.

- *Recognising feelings: Facial Bingo* – strengthens pupils' understanding of strong feelings, both their own and others. It enables them to further develop a language for feelings, to know where and how to get help with their feelings, to share their feelings and help themselves.

- *Understanding feelings: body feelings* – the focus is to strengthen pupils' understanding of strong feelings, both their own and others. It enables them to further develop a language for feelings, to know where and how to get help with their feelings, to share their feelings and help themselves.

- *Gauging our feelings* – aims to help pupils talk about and reflect on the different feelings they may experience in a variety of situations.

- *Developing positive coping strategies* – aims to help pupils recognise a range of emotions in other people and to identify who and how to ask for help with emotions that may feel challenging. This helps pupils to develop a wide range of strategies for managing feelings and emotions positively.

Organisation: PSHE

Source: www.pshe-association.org.uk/system/files/Secondary%20lesson%20plans_0.pdf

Target: Key stages 3, 4

What: Secondary resources

- *Promoting emotional health during transition into key stage* – understanding the concept of support network and who to turn to when worried.

- *Promoting emotional wellbeing* – different core lessons for different key stages on understanding and promoting emotional wellbeing.

- *Resilience and reframing failure* – the focus is on what is meant by resilience; the role of resilience in success; what we mean by failure; being able to reframe and learn from failure.

- *Unhealthy coping strategies: self-harm* – the lesson enables students to feel more comfortable talking about self-harm; to understand that self-harm is an unhealthy coping strategy and to identify some of the things that might trigger it; to know the signs to look out for in a friend; to know where and how to get support for themselves or a friend.

- *Unhealthy coping strategies: eating disorders* – the lesson is structured to enable students to feel more comfortable talking about eating disorders; to know the signs to look out for in a friend; to know where and how to get support for themselves or a friend.

- *Understanding and managing depression and anxiety* – the lesson enables students to feel more comfortable talking about depression and anxiety; to know the signs to look out for in a friend; to know where and how to get support for themselves or a friend.

- *Healthy coping strategies* – this lesson will enable students to recognise a range of difficult emotions; to identify a range of strategies for managing difficult emotions; to know where and how to access further support.

- *Mindfulness* – this lesson will enable students to know what mindfulness is; to explain how it might benefit them; to practise mindfulness; to know how to incorporate mindfulness into their daily routine.

Lessons such as these are likely to result in an increase in disclosures, so it is important to make sure you are familiar with the school's safeguarding policy and procedures for managing disclosures. The PSHE Association has produced guidance on talking to students when they make mental health disclosures. Consider any sensitivities and prior knowledge about specific students' circumstances. Where you are aware of any relevant issues, it may be advisable to give prior notice that this subject will be covered. Notice should be given to pastoral staff in the school, and details of local support groups or helplines should also be made available for further support after the lesson.[1]

---

1   See PSHE Association (July 2015) *Supplement to Guidance Document: Preparing to Teach About Mental Health and Emotional Wellbeing, Lesson Plans for Key Stages 3 and 4*.

Key guidance when talking about self-harm

This is a subject that needs very careful handling and should always be taught in line with best practice principles, as outlined in the guidance document. In this lesson, it is important not to talk about specific ways in which people harm themselves or ways in which people might hide their self-harm, as this could provide instruction to any vulnerable pupils in the room. (PSHE Association, *Supplement to Guidance Document: Preparing to Teach About Mental Health and Emotional Wellbeing, Lesson Plans for Key Stages 3 and 4*, July 2015)

Key guidance when talking about eating disorders

This is a subject that needs very careful handling and should always be taught in line with best practice principles, as outlined in the guidance document. In this lesson, it is important not to talk about specific ways in which people lose weight, purge or hide eating disorder symptoms, as this could provide instruction to any vulnerable pupils in the room. It is also important not to discuss numbers when discussing weight loss, or to share extreme images, as this can provide a 'benchmark' or aspirational example for vulnerable young people. (PSHE Association, *Supplement to Guidance Document: Preparing to Teach About Mental Health and Emotional Wellbeing, Lesson Plans for Key Stages 3 and 4*, July 2015)

Organisation: British Association for Counselling and Psychotherapy

Source: www.thegrid.org.uk/learning/hwb/ewb/resources/documents/exploring_mental_health_14-16yr_olds.pdf

Target: Students aged 14–16

What:

- *Words, Stereotypes and Feeling* – students are asked to consider their own feelings and those of others in relation to the language explored.

- *Myths and Reality* – these activities encourage discussion around attitudes and knowledge.

- *Stigma* – asks students to begin to experience what stigma is.

- *What Causes a Mental Health Problem* – asks students to explore those factors which might have a negative and sometimes debilitating effect on a person's emotional health and wellbeing.

- *Risk and Resilience* – helps students to explore risk and resilience factors and perhaps privately relate them to their own experience.

- *Emotional Health and Wellbeing* – encourages students to explore what might constitute emotional health and its counterpart, unhealthy functioning.

- *Mental Illness and Young People* – invites students to begin to understand the range of mental health problems faced by young people.

- *Feelings and Behaviour* – students are asked to explore how mental health difficulties might affect a young person at school.

- *Feelings, Mental Health and Learning* – the connection: calls on students to understand these concepts and relate them to personal experience.

- *Who Can Help* – helps students explore the possibilities of where they can get help.

- *A Listening Ear* – encourages students to develop the skills of helping but also to understand when it may be necessary to involve adults.

- *Communicating What We Feel* – encourages students to develop an extended feelings vocabulary and to use it in their daily lives.

- *A Mentally Healthy School* – asks students to identify ways in which schools already do this and how emotional health can further be supported.

- *Questions in a Box* – these final activities offer the class an opportunity to ask questions and explore feelings.

Organisation: Samaritans

Source: www.samaritans.org/your-community/samaritans-education/deal-developing-emotional-awareness-and-listening

Target: Key stages 3, 4; 14 years

What: DEAL (Developing Emotional Awareness and Listening) is a free teaching resource aimed at students aged approximately 14 and over and has excellent digital and film and audio resources to accompany the lessons:

- *Emotional health.*

- *Coping strategies.*

- *Dealing with feelings.*

- *Connecting with others and communication skills.*

Organisation: Time to Change

Source: www.time-to-change.org.uk/get-involved/get-involved-schools/school-resources

Target: Key stages 2, 3, 4

What:

- *Ten-minute assemblies and 15-minute assemblies and campaign toolkits.*

- *Leadership and campaigning guide.*

- *Shorter activities* – Mental Health Spectrum; Mental Health Quiz; Mental Health v. Mental Illness – Graffiti Wall; Conversation Bingo; Conversation Starter Game.

- *Posters and leaflets* – young person's leaflet and poster – print onto A3 paper; parents' leaflet and poster – print onto A3 paper; top tip cards; Stand Up Kid poster; screensaver.

- *Resources for parents* – open letter written by a parent of a young person with experience of mental health problems; short presentation on mental health in children and young people; leaflet on talking about mental health.

You can also create, customise and download your own resources.

Organisation: Cornwall Healthy Schools

Source: www.cornwallhealthyschools.org/wellbeing/ss-mh

Target: Year 9

What: STOP Stigma is a resource which aims to increase Year 9 students' awareness of stigma linked to mental health problems and the role of language in stigmatisation, and to reduce stigma by increasing students' knowledge and understanding of mental health problems. Excellent links and video resources support this scheme of work.

- *Attitudes and Knowledge Survey.*

- *Awareness of Mental Illness and Stigma.*

- *Facts and Myths about Mental Health* – how myths and negative attitudes to mental health contribute to stigma.

- *Wellbeing and Normalising Mental Health.*

- *Learning More about Specific Mental Health Problems.*

- *Creating and Running an Anti-Stigma Campaign.*

Organisation: Charlie Waller Memorial Trust YouTube channel

Source: www.youtube.com/channel/UCPJauIgUy_B9N1BAI-N7A2Q/videos

Target: Teachers and some videos for students

What: A collection of videos giving brief and punchy explanations covering a range of topics:

- Anxiety, self-harm, depression, eating disorders, body image and a host of videos and webinars for the teacher and the lead on mental wellbeing.

Organisation: Gaia Technologies

Source: Google Playstore to purchase either Gaia Young Mind or Gaia TeenMind

Target: Key stage 2 and 3

What: Covering a range of issues associated with Personal, social, health and economic (PSHE) education. The content is designed to appeal to different age ranges. These Apps provide users with advice, information and points of contact on all subjects to do with wellbeing.

- My Body: body image, eating disorders, healthy eating, puberty, sex and gender.

- My Mind: depression, self-harm, stress, anxiety.

- My Relationships: bullying, peer pressure, sexting.

- My Relaxation: a mindfulness breathing feature.

- A Mood Tracker: where users can record their daily moods to identify recurring patterns and coping strategies.

10

Create Safe Spaces for Wellbeing Support

KEY POINTS

* Students need to have 'spaces' in the school, open every day, for self-referral if they feel they need additional support.

* Staff and peers who provide support in these rooms should be trained on how to listen and how to spot the signs, and safeguarding procedures for any disclosures.

* Combine the pop-up wellbeing spaces and curricular spaces: academic space in lesson time; wellbeing space at lunchtime.

In our schools, we are very strong on advising, telling and instructing young people how they should behave, react and respond but we appear to be less effective at just listening.

As mentioned in an earlier chapter, we conducted primary research to ascertain the mental wellbeing barometer of our students. The response was that most students wanted face-to-face support but did not know where to go, who to talk to and when they could go.

Secondary schools are an interesting space – often three or four times the size of the local primary schools and packed with over 1000 young people. Couple this with the teenage developmental challenges where they are neither child nor adult and are often going through an extraordinary combination of vulnerability and intense feelings, and the school setting can be a heady cocktail mix of emotions. For some young people, school is a sensory overload, a battleground of having to navigate friendships and choices and it's an achievement that they even made it to school. It is a 'big ask' to expect 1000+ young people to cope all of the time and for everyone to be happy and getting along.

We cannot ignore the fact at some point in a young person's journey through secondary school things may not be all okay and if they can't talk to their parents, often the best people to support this will be their peers or their teacher, who see the student daily.

We need 'safe spaces' in our schools to facilitate this kind of support. A 'safe space' in a school is a place where they have some control over what happens next; a place where for a few moments they can press pause and gather their emotions; a place where they feel less threatened and overwhelmed by what is happening; a place where if they want to talk to someone without fear of being judged, or even exposed, they can.

But how can this be incorporated when schools have six lessons a day and are trying to maximise their academic learning time with the young people?

I believe pop-up safe spaces can easily operate at lunchtimes and in classrooms, using trained peers and teaching staff, and should have a range of purposes dependent on the needs in your school community. Below are a few examples of different spaces I have seen trialled effectively in various schools.

Most schools do not have a budget to build a separate space, so you have to be quite canny and combine the wellbeing zone with curricular spaces. For example: for six periods a day they are teaching classrooms spaces but when it is lunch or break they become part of the wellbeing zone or pop-up spaces. To achieve this, you don't need a massive change in decoration, you just need clever signposting.

- *The Pop-In Q Zone* – based on an invitation only from staff, this space is where some of the most vulnerable students who are facing daily 'challenges' can just 'hang out' at lunch in a sensory quiet zone. These may be children who find navigating lunch and social times difficult. They may be young people with diagnosed conditions like Asperger's syndrome or they may even be young people on the child protection register. It is totally optional for these young people to stay in this room. They can be referred by any staff member. In the room, there are mindful colouring-in books, spirographs, chess, Minecraft in creative mode and various board games for them to play. It is a happy room to hang out in, with a genuine bubbly atmosphere as the young people clearly feel safe and they have a space where they belong, where they are valued. In this room, you will also find wellbeing and anti-bullying peer mentors ready to chat and listen to anyone who looks as if they are struggling or even just lonely.

- *The Pop-In Wellbeing Room* – students can come here to talk about personal issues that they are facing and have a trained wellbeing ambassador (some schools use the charity Relate for training) to listen without judgement and to signpost support in and outside school. This is an effective space to quickly triage if a young person is facing more complex mental wellbeing challenges.

- *The Pop-In Antibullying Room* – this is where students can come and talk about complaints of bullying or even just breakdown in friendship communication. Reports can be filed and investigated and day-to-day peer mentoring and signposting can take place, helping the young person find the best way forward. Restorative sessions can take place here too. This is where the two parties can share their version of the event and tell the truth about how they felt and what motivated them. Thus, encouraging from both parties accountability, acknowledging harm done and their role in the incident. By agreeing a way forward this gives them a personal stake in the success of their future relationship.

- *The Pop-In GSA (Gay–Straight Alliance)* or *Freedom to Be Space* – this is a student-led movement where the goal of most gay–straight alliances is to make their school community safe by challenging homophobia and homophobic language and create a welcoming environment for LGBT students and their straight allies in a regular lunchtime meeting space. This is a great space for breaking down barriers and encouraging a school community to create a culture of respect.

- *The Pop-In YC Space* – young carers can gather here and can find support from staff and solidarity with other young carers as they cope with the demands of their responsibilities. Sometimes a sympathetic or supportive chat can make a huge difference to the young carer. Sometimes they don't need to chat but it just needs to be recognised with a smile that they are doing an amazing job. It also enables the schools to be more vigilant and help track the wellbeing of their young carers and spot any warning signs or concerning trends.

The location of the 'wellbeing zone' or safe space matters. It is important that it is seen as something separate from the SEN space because we need to publicly recognise that having a mental wellbeing challenge does not always equate with having a learning need. It needs to be destigmatised in schools and given its own 'public' signposting and space. Otherwise, many of the children who are facing challenges won't come and visit as they don't see themselves as having a learning need.

On the issue of discreetness, we found the only things stopping young people from using these spaces are trust and not knowing what will happen when they come into the room. I always advise my student ambassadors and staff to give assemblies talking about these rooms – removing the mystique of what they are here for and breaking down what will happen into user-friendly chunks of information. It is important that these spaces do what they say they will do and that they deliver on their promise. Soon, news will travel by word of mouth through the school that these are spaces that genuinely do help students and help make their lives a bit better.

Finally, all spaces allow students to feel connected, valued, heard and safe. Some visit the zones or spaces regularly. Others may only use one of the rooms once or twice in their school years. Others may never use them. What is important is that they all know they are always there for them or a peer should they need them. It is this assurance which helps enormously with the pre-emptive support we aim to give regarding the mental wellbeing of our students.

11

Referrals and Mental Wellbeing Mentors

KEY POINTS

* A school should operate on two levels for students needing/ seeking support with their mental wellbeing: student self-referral and staff referral.

* Easy-to-complete referral forms are vital for student mentors to record the conversation. Make sure these are filed confidentially.

* I always advise my students ambassadors and staff to give assemblies talking about these rooms.

A school should operate on two levels for students needing/ seeking support with their mental wellbeing: student self-referral and staff referral. At the end of each referral process should be a trained wellbeing student ambassador and a trained adult.

The pop-in safe rooms at lunchtime can act as safe spaces for students to self-refer, encouraging students to help themselves. The respective peer ambassadors supporting in the rooms should be trained to listen with empathy; to not pre-judge; to acknowledge the person's feelings; to listen and provide moral support; to write everything down so the school has a record;

and to signpost where they can get further help in the school. It is also vital that they are trained to make clear how the information will be handled in terms of confidentiality and to ensure safeguarding, and that the young person is invited back the next day to carry on the conversation and identify strategies for coping.

Tracking and recording

Easy-to-complete referral forms are vital for student mentors to record the conversation. Make sure these are filed confidentially. It is the responsibility of the teacher on duty in the rooms to check this file daily and ensure that the information is acted on. For example, in the anti-bullying room, a template is used to record a bullying report and it's important that the relevant tutors are made aware so that they can investigate the bullying reports and the situation can be dealt with quickly. The anti-bullying ambassadors are there to support all the children involved and to basically be a peer supporter for them while the report is being investigated by the adults. *It is not the place of the anti-bullying ambassador to investigate and decide.* Similarly, with the wellbeing ambassadors in the other rooms mentioned, their role is to *listen* and document what is shared, making sure it is brought to the attention of staff.

Referral flow chart

The room where students are sent if it is a staff referral is not usually a classroom – it is a specially designed room for individual support by appointment only. It should be operated by adult mental wellbeing mentors, preferably also trained as mental health first aiders. Having a robust internal referral chart for staff to follow helps ensure clarity with the steps teachers can take. It also helps all staff know that they need to try some interventions first. If the student referred has been clearly identified as facing mental wellbeing challenges, then they could be placed on an intervention programme which seeks to provide one of the following:

- one-to-one supportive sessions, which have an agreed time span over a period of weeks
- self-esteem and confidence-building programmes[1]
- an opportunity to explore and develop problem-solving skills
- the setting up of specific support programmes with specialist external agencies
- guidance, advice and information on where they can get further support
- if necessary, referral to CAMHS.

Note: Chapter 14 How to Make Interventions Work has more detail on effective mental wellbeing interventions.

The adult mental wellbeing mentors should discuss with the students and their parents the appropriate support to ensure that the student keeps attending school and feels safe enough to remain motivated, and confident enough to stay focused on their learning. The mentors should also aim to work in collaboration with the SEN and pastoral support teams, sharing information, and providing students with reasonable adjustments under an individual student support mental wellbeing plan. This plan should identify:

- the nature of the need
- the programme and person they will be working with
- the strategies identified to support the young person

---

1   I would recommend getting a copy of Deborah Plummer's *Helping Children to Build Self-Esteem* (2007) and *Helping Adolescents and Adults to Build Self-Esteem* (2014), both published by Jessica Kingsley Publishers, London.

- the time allocated for interventions

- outcomes and impact.

This is a crucial stage because information needs to be clearly shared so that all key stakeholders know what they are doing. In one school, they simply used an Excel spreadsheet which was internally shared and updated with key information. I have found software called *Provision Mapping* helpful as it has an interface which allows you to fill and track all the necessary details about the intervention plan. Ideally, you would want the information all in one place, and if schools are using SIMS then all intervention and tracking data is in one place – the same place where you would register attendance and log behaviour details. What is important is that schools are proactive and not reactive.

Contacting the parents is also essential. School pastoral leads and mental wellbeing mentors must not make any decision without consulting parents and students. They are key because if they don't buy-in to your intervention programme then it is very top down and prescriptive.

It is not just the responsibility of the student wellbeing ambassadors or the adult mentors to support mental wellbeing. All staff have the responsibility of being mental wellbeing gatekeepers and need to be trained in how to spot the warning signs. They are expected to reach out as caring human beings and speak up if they have concerns about a student, and signpost where help can be sought.

12

Harness the Power of Peer Mentoring

KEY POINTS

* Train the student ambassadors properly. This is about safeguarding.

* Set up a formal application process giving it the gravitas it deserves.

* Recognise the ambassadors with easily identifiable coats/clothes/badges and set up a rota where they are in the pop-up space and in the playground. Make them visible to all.

Peer mentoring is without a doubt the most effective resource in any school's wellbeing programme. I have witnessed five years of work where a peer mentoring scheme has had the capacity and power to reach out to the whole school, producing active citizens and bringing about real change through persistent public campaign work, which I explain in the example below.

My journey into understanding the power of peer mentoring all started with a group of my media students who produced the groundbreaking film, *Homophobia – our closeted education*,[1] which went on to educate thousands of students and teachers up

---

1   https://vimeo.com/128591375.

and down the country and get a special mention in the House of Commons.

The students were driven by a conviction that homophobic language should not be tolerated in our school. It soon became apparent they wanted to be more than just media students – they wanted to stand up and promote their message; they wanted to educate the ignorant; to listen and signpost support for the victims; to make sure the staff were trained, educated and supporting this anti-bullying ideology; to be pre-emptive in their support and prevent homophobia from having a breeding ground in our school. In short, they were 'inspirational'. Thanks to a UK anti-bullying charity called The Diana Award,[2] we discovered an anti-bullying ambassadors programme running in schools. We tapped into its comprehensive training and education programmes and this is how these media students became our first cohort of anti-bullying ambassadors. I had truly experienced the power of the student voice.

After the success of the anti-bullying ambassadors, it seemed a natural progression to build a wellbeing ambassadors programme. To truly make this programme effective they need to be trained properly. For the programme, I used the services of Relate West Surrey,[3] which delivered an impressive 15 hours of training in peer listening and mental wellbeing. We raised the funds for this via our school county and local council, and it was money well spent. Since then, I have seen schools use local counsellors to deliver the training in how to listen and signpost; Mental Health First Aid (MHFA)[4] delivers powerful and effective training too, ranging from half-day to two-day courses.

For *all* the safe spaces in your wellbeing zone to be successful, they need to be led by the students themselves, which means that each space needs to have *all* peer mentors trained in how to listen and in safeguarding, referring and signposting. When it

---

2   https://diana-award.org.uk.
3   http://relatewestsurrey.org.uk.
4   https://mhfaengland.org/individuals/youth/half-day.

comes to recruiting participants and setting up your peer mentoring, there are a few crucial steps I would encourage you to adopt, which I detail below.

Pitch and sell the concept

Pitch for applications to be submitted in a high-profile assembly presentation to your Year 10 students. Make sure a very senior member of staff pitches and explains the programme and what it means for the school. Give it the gravitas it deserves and stress that to be selected is an achievement. Bring back the 'cool' factor in being a role model…in being an upstander…in being a wellbeing champion…in being a young citizen who champions equality, care and compassion and wants to be proactive about building a better society for all.

Keep an open mind about the application process

Ask students to submit applications on one page, so they can explain why they want this role, why they think they are suitable and what difference they think they could make to the programme. The interesting point to note here is that it is not always the top academic student and most well-behaved student who make the best ambassadors. Sometimes the best ambassadors come from the students who have already walked the road of being bullied, being a bully, suffering from mental health challenges or have a family member who is living with a diagnosed mental health disability or illness. These students are often unknown to staff or have had an interesting track record. I never judge. Every student is welcome to apply. Don't refuse a student because of their prior track record – if they have been brave enough to come forward in spite of what has gone on before, they might make a well-informed and courageous ambassador.

Be serious about the training

Set up a training programme. Take students out of lessons if it is half- or full-day training. Bring in external specialists to help train the students. They need to be fully briefed on the subject matter, their role, safeguarding and following school policy and procedures. If you get this right, the students will feel confident about their role and empowered to act – the rest will fall into place.

Train the anti-bullying ambassadors

Anti-bullying ambassadors need to be trained in understanding the Equality Act 2010 and what this means as a piece of legislation in our society. The also need to understand:

- their own subliminal bias in what a victim or bully looks like and realise it could be anyone

- what the role of an ambassador is

- how to take down a factual report and support an emotional young person who comes into the room to file a report

- how to identify a safeguarding scenario and how to respond, ensuring safeguarding procedures are followed without hesitation

- how to ensure that the anti-bullying ambassador is supported and has someone to talk to.

Train the wellbeing ambassadors

Wellbeing ambassadors need training in the concept of mental wellbeing as a continuum and mental wellbeing challenges they may come across in a school setting, such as anxiety, stress, domestic–home life problems, self-harm, eating disorders and relationship problems. They need to be trained in:

- non-judgemental listening and to look at the power of body language (keeping eye contact, open body stance, non-threatening position when listening)

- how to ask questions to check understanding of what has been said, and summarising facts and feelings

- how to sit with silence and not feel they must finish sentences, give solutions or compare with an anecdote of their own

- the difference between empathy and sympathy

- how to identify a safeguarding concern when they feel the young person or someone else may be at real risk of harm

- how to ensure that the young person knows that seldom is it completely confidential and that there will always be an adult in the room at least who will be aware of the content of the conversation

- how to refer to the adult wellbeing mentors for further one-to-one intervention

- how to ensure that the ambassadors themselves are supported and have someone to talk to each week if they feel distressed by anything they have heard.

Don't try to fix it

What is vital is that all ambassadors are trained to realise that their role is not to 'fix it' and not to attempt to or promise they can. Their role is to be that point of contact for another young person who might prefer to talk to them rather than a teacher and that they are there to help the young person help themselves. In training , I suggest they could say, 'I cannot fix this for you, but I can walk next to you while you get this sorted. We are here, every lunchtime to listen, support, guide, have lunch with you. You are not alone. We care.'

Duties and bling

The ambassadors are students themselves and often have their own school and extra-curricular activities. As they are volunteers, I try to ensure that they can find days which suit them and there is flexibility in the duty rota. I encourage ambassadors to give up two half lunchtime sessions. They are always on duty with another ambassador. The first duty is walkabout duty at lunchtimes, particularly in the play areas where the younger students hang out, and the second duty is in the designated pop-in room that the school has allocated. At all times, the students need to wear something that easily identifies them as an ambassador – it could be a coat, armband, a tie.

There needs to be a probation period after training where you can trial out the students to see if they attend all their duties, they feel comfortable in this role and they are role models in and outside school. There are always one or two students who pull out because they don't feel comfortable. This is totally fine, and they should be applauded for being honest, not be made to feel that they did not 'make it'. Knowing our own limitations is a strength.

After a one-month probation, we give out the badges. This is done again in assembly, emphasising the gravitas of what they have achieved. It also sets up aspirations for the younger years to want to be like these young people when they are in Year 10.

Finally, the words of one student who spoke at a youth mental wellbeing and wellbeing TeachMeet[5] capture the essence of this youth drive and passion:

> I wanted to help students who feel the same way I once felt. I wanted for young teens to be able to have one person who would listen to their problems, like I wish I did. And knowing personally how much that can help someone get out of such a dark and desolate space drives me more.

5   A TeachMeet is an organised but informal meeting where teachers gather to share and demonstrate good practice to other colleagues. The events are free and open to all.

13

Embrace Digital Technology

KEY POINTS

* Set up a page on your school website with suitable websites for students, parents and staff to visit.

* Ensure all digital information provided is filtered for relevance and suitability.

* Don't just reply on apps. Apps are best used in conjunction with other forms of therapy and support (YoungMinds).

Mental illness is complex and can be enduring. Marjorie Wallace, Chief Executive of SANE, says, 'It's like living in a house of paper. Too much is seen, too much is heard. Too many shadows and too many voices.'[1] It can also have an impact on carers, family and friends. It's important schools signpost to the young people and their families where they can get additional support.

There are some excellent websites with succinct and relevant material and I would strongly urge schools to have a list of these on the school website as they are useful for parents and students to access.

---

1   www.sane.org.uk/what_we_do/about_sane.

- *www.cwmt.org* – The Charlie Waller Memorial Trust charity helps equip young people to look after their mental wellbeing. It has been set up to help people to recognise the signs of depression in themselves and others, so they know when to seek help. The charity delivers workshops and talks to young people and those who work with them about how to stay mentally well and it has excellent self-help resources for schools to use.

- *www.sane.org.uk* – SANE is committed to raising public awareness and research, and bringing more effective professional treatment and compassionate care to everyone affected by mental illness. SANE offers emotional support and information to anyone affected by mental health problems through its helpline and online Support Forum, where people share their feelings and experiences. It has a national out-of-hours helpline (Saneline 0300 304 7000, 4.30pm to 10.30pm daily), which provides support and information to anyone coping with mental illness.

- *www.minded.org.uk* – MindEd is suitable for all adults working with, or caring for, infants, children or teenagers. All the information provided is quality assured by experts, and is useful and easy to understand. It aims to give adults who care for, or work with, young people:

  - the knowledge to support their wellbeing

  - the understanding to identify a child at risk of a mental health condition

  - the confidence to act on their concern and, if needed, signpost to services that can help.

- *www.mind.org.uk* – Mind has worked to improve the lives of all people with experience of mental health problems. It has more than 1000 services, such as supported housing, crisis helplines, drop-in centres, employment and training schemes, counselling and befriending.

- *www.youngminds.org.uk* – YoungMinds is a leading charity fighting for young people's mental health. The YoungMinds resources library is full of useful toolkits, publications, reports and policy information about children and young people's mental health. There is also a YoungMinds parent helpline (0808 802 5544), which offers free confidential online and phone support to parents/guardians worried about the behaviour and mental health of a young person.

- *www.mindful.org* – Mindful celebrates mindfulness, awareness and compassion in all aspects of life, through *Mindful* magazine, events and collaborations. It offers examples for simple mindful practices for daily life, coping with anxiety, how to recognise your inner critic, and gratitude practices.

- *www.anxietyuk.org.uk* – Anxiety UK helps all those suffering with anxiety disorders. It has an information line number (08444 775 774) where you can talk to someone in complete confidence between 9.30am and 5.30pm, Monday to Friday. This site offers good resources for young people living with anxiety.

- *www.selfharm.co.uk* – SelfharmUK is a project dedicated to supporting young people impacted by self-harm, providing a safe space to talk, ask any questions and be honest about what's going on in your life. The site helps with facts, myths, staying safe and useful links to sites to find additional support.

- *www.anorexiabulimiacare.org.uk* – ABC is a national UK eating disorders organisation with over 25 years of experience. It provides ongoing care, emotional support and practical guidance for anyone affected by eating disorders, those struggling personally and parents, families and friends. ABC works to increase awareness and understanding of eating disorders through talks, training and campaigns for change. Telephone helplines are open from 9.30am to 5.30pm Monday–Friday.

- *www.youthhealthtalk.org* – This site has helpful video clips of people in same situation sharing their mental health experiences, advice and support. There is a section on young people talking about their experiences of depression and eating disorders.

- *www.thecalmzone.net* – CALM (Campaign Against Men Living Miserably) is a charity targeted at young men aged 15–35. It has a helpline (0800 585858) and a website set up to support young men in response to the high suicide rate among this group.

- www.childline.org.uk – Childline is a 24-hour online or phone helpline (0800 1111) offering a free and confidential advice and counselling service for parents, children and young people.

As useful as it may seem having these websites on your school website, it does not, however, necessarily help the young person in question. When we conducted research into the mental wellbeing barometer in one school, it was clear that students were overwhelmed by how much material there is online and the need to sift and sort through it; they often felt the advice offered online was a lot for them to navigate through and they became rapidly despondent.

So, the question remains – will the students know where to go for additional help and support?

For most year groups when we asked, 'Do you know where to get support?', the same answers were coming up: young people were unsure, in their own school and local community, where to get help, when was the best time to seek help and who they should contact.

The problem was further compounded as we discovered that teachers did not feel they had the right training or language to discuss mental wellbeing issues facing the teenagers in their classes. For example, many teachers have said to me that they are uncomfortable having to talk about challenges like self-harm or eating disorders or sexual orientation as they don't feel they know enough about these subjects and are worried they will say the wrong thing and make matters worse.

It appeared that what was needed was accessible platforms giving out clear and relevant information to our young people, their parents *and* to our teachers.

We needed a 24-hour platform which covered the basic definition, signs to look out for, advice and bespoke signposting to where to get help in our school and our community. But the question was how? A traditional poster? Leaflets? On the school website?

We asked the young people, who said they wanted something that was quick and accessible. Knowing that their smartphones represent the most popular platform for young people for anything from social life to information gathering, building an app was the obvious choice. It was clear we needed to embrace digital technology when addressing mental wellbeing and support for young people.

A case study: *Brighton Hill TeenMind*

The *Brighton Hill TeenMind* app was conceived as a piece of mental wellbeing cross-curricular coursework with Year 9 mixed ability media students in one school and then evolved further with wellbeing ambassadors from another school. It seemed to make sense to build a bespoke mental wellbeing app in our school for our students and teachers, which was free to use, always available and was mostly an information-giving tool. Basically, we did the sifting and sorting for the students, teachers and parents so they had all the information in the palm of their hand when having a conversation about an aspect of a young person's mental wellbeing.

I was delighted when Gaia Technologies – a leading, provider of ICT products and solutions to education institutions – said it was willing to work with our students on the condition that the students led the design work and the content for the project. Perfect. Another example of ensuring student voice and further empowering the young people to make sure that the support put in place was commensurate with their needs.

I was able to create a cross-curricular scheme of work around the topic 'App Design', which I delivered to my Year 9, mixed-ability media students over the autumn term. After we had researched the industry we began to look at our product and target audience and I got them to question what would be relevant to their age group when it came to mental and emotional support. They researched NHS and related mental wellbeing online resources available to teens, both on websites and in other apps, and quickly set about designing a product with content that met their needs. They were, after all, the target audience!

Because of the nature of the content and to ensure safeguarding procedures were adhered to, before any content was published it was double checked by mental wellbeing charity Woking Mind, mental wellbeing nurses, social workers, safeguarding leads and educational professionals.

A popular feature is the mood tracker, which allows users to track their daily moods and enable reflection on any patterns they see occurring and possible triggers. This feature has been a 'way in' for tutors, parents and peers to start discussions with students showing concerning signs.

Four main themes were identified with many subsections:

- My Body

    » Body image

    » Eating disorders

    » Healthy eating

    » Puberty

    » Sex and gender

- My Mind

    » Depression

    » Self-harm

    » Stress

- My Relationships

    » Bullying

    » Friendship

» Peer pressure and sexting

» Sex and consent

- My.Relaxation (a series of mindfulness breathing exercises)

» Grounded breathing

» Grounded breathing and complete breath

» Physical and breath awareness.

In each section, there are short definitions, signs to look out for, advice and where to get help in the school and the community.

By using this app, teachers, parents and students now have the language to start the essential discussions with our students about mental wellbeing. For example, a student referred another student to a teacher because she was concerned about her self-harming. The young girl in question had distinct scratch marks on her arm and admitted to doing it. The teacher knew now was the time to have that first conversation but was not sure where to start. She quickly accessed the app and suggested that they looked up a bit of information together about self-harm.

They read the *definition* together and discussed if that felt accurate to the young person in question. They read the section on *signs to look out for* and the young person was able to identify some common signs – this was important because it validated what she was feeling. They together read the *advice* section and discussed some of the advice given and what the young person felt might be relevant. They then looked at the *signposting* section on where and who she could go to for support.

By using the app, the teacher, without much trouble, had a sound conversation with the young person about her recent self-harming. The teacher had not passed it on or referred it – thus delaying the intervention – but instead made the most of the moment and the strong relationship she had with the young person. The young person felt listened to and validated. The teacher was able to now record the conversation and ensure that the young person was tracked and supported using her network of relationships around her, like her family and friends.

However, just downloading the app and having it on the student's phone does not mean we are properly raising awareness and helping these young people make informed choices should the situation arise for them in the future.

We need to ensure that the young people properly explore it so that they know what is out there for them, when they need it. As a result, seven PSHE (personal, social and health education) lessons have been written around the app encouraging young people to explore scenarios for fictitious characters to help them identify their challenges and which aspects of the app would be most useful. The PSHE lessons are proving to be very effective with the 11– and 12-year-olds (Year 7).

So, what is the impact? The app has been gratefully received by teachers, parents and wellbeing ambassadors. The reason for its success is that it gives everyone something to work from when having a conversation about one of the topics about a young person's mental wellbeing. In fact the app, Brighton Hill TeenMind was nominated as a BETT 2019 Finalist for the category of IMPACT to education. If you want explore how to customise the app for your school, then visit these sites:

- Gaia TeenMind – www.computingframework.co.uk/product/secondary-gaia-teen-mind

- Gaia YoungMind – www.computingframework.co.uk/product/primary-gaia-young-mind.

What can schools do if they can't create the app?

It might be a good idea to create a mental health and wellbeing page on your school website and create Definition/Advice/Where can I get help tabs for students, parents and staff to refer to. In this way, you can always refer to these pages on your website.

Note: There are plenty of apps out there now for young people to access but as the YoungMinds charity noted on its pages, many mental wellbeing apps and online programmes lack 'an underlying evidence base' and have 'a lack of scientific credibility and limited clinical effectiveness'. Many experts suggest that apps are best used in conjunction with other forms of therapy and support. It's always best to talk to a GP or a trusted adult mental wellbeing professional about the app you are using and get a second opinion.

14

How to Make Interventions Work

KEY POINTS

* For the student facing mental health challenges, if there is nothing happening in their lives that they seem interested in then encourage them to join or get the school to create an extra-curricular club or sport for them to take part in.

* Different types of intervention will suit different students. Work to the strengths of the teachers and local community.

* It is essential to build relationships with the student and get them to have a greater awareness of their strengths and the resources available to them.

The March 2016 UK Government advice for schools states:

> ...the intervention of the school can be the turning point. Having a 'sense of connectedness' or belonging to a school is a recognised protective factor for mental health. Activities that bolster mental health operate under a variety of headings, including 'emotional literacy', 'emotional intelligence', 'resilience', 'character and grit', 'life skills', 'violence prevention', 'anti-bullying', and 'coping skills'. Systematic reviews of this work show that the best of interventions, when well implemented, are

effective in both promoting positive mental health for all, and targeting those with problems.[1]

School educators need to recognise that a young person whose behaviour – whether it is disruptive, withdrawn, anxious, depressed or otherwise – may be related to an unmet mental wellbeing need. Furthermore, that this mental wellbeing challenge could be supported with pre-emptive and proactive interventions.

Some school educators may put up a degree of resistance to running interventions in the school day as the young person may miss lessons. However, it is important to keep in mind the following points about running effective intervention programmes:

- Intervention programmes are not a threat to academic performance; rather, they're there to support and enhance the student's progress through their academic journey. They are part of the 'inclusive' education all schools should be delivering so that every child can flourish.

- Intervention programmes are not random 'hit and miss' ideas but represent a specific part of the student's education health plan – well researched, tailor made and specific to a student's needs at that phase in their life, and often utilising expert external support.

- Interventions offered by the school can be the turning point in promoting the resilience of their students. Having a 'sense of connectedness' or belonging to a school is a recognised protective factor for mental wellbeing.

- Being pre-emptive and proactive and addressing issues early will most definitely limit problems later.

We need to be confident and supportive of the power of early intervention programmes. If they are specific to the student's

---

1   *Mental Health and Behaviour in Schools: Departmental advice for school staff* (March 2016) London: Department for Education, p.19.

needs, time bonded, closely tracked and data driven to measure impact, these programmes can serve to empower and give the young person the confidence and growth mindset to carry on.

What do effective interventions look like?

It's important to carefully consider the young person and find the right intervention for their needs.

Interventions can range in format: self-refer lunchtime safe spaces; staff referral interventions either one-to-one or in group situations; cross-curricular in lessons or with teacher; after-school, extra-curricular, pop-up-style interventions.

Self-refer lunchtime safe spaces

Having a wellbeing pop-in room with trained staff and wellbeing peer ambassadors ready to listen is an important intervention all schools could be encouraged to adopt. Just being secure in the knowledge that the space and resource is there for a young person to pop in and use – should they need it – to have the conversation, is an important type of intervention for the young person to choose to use. It also encourages resilience as they are proactive in looking at the strategies and support available to them.

Staff referral interventions either one-to-one or in group situations

Here students can receive:

- one-to-one supportive sessions, which have an agreed time span, over a period of weeks

- self-esteem and confidence-building programmes

- an opportunity to explore and develop problem-solving skills

- specific support programmes set up with mental health support teams[2] (as pledged in the updated version of the UK government's *Transforming Children and Young People's Mental Health Provision*) provided by local council and specialist external agencies related to, for example, anxiety, grief, trauma, eating disorders, substance misuse

- guidance, advice and information on where they can get further support

- if necessary, conversations with parents and referral to CAMHS.

While we wait for the much-promised mental health support teams and finance to trickle down into schools and budgets, the key is to access and tap into 'free' intervention programmes from external agencies. For example, tapping into counsellors who have completed training but need to volunteer a certain number of hours before they qualify is a good route.

Sometimes charities have already obtained funding from lottery, county or CAMHS/NHS sources and it is about tapping into these programmes for your school. In Surrey, a school made use of a charity called East to West, as well as CAMHS Youth Advisors and CYP Havens, who were superb with supporting individual students and their families with specialist CAMHS support, youth support and peer mentor input. You can find out who the youth and mental health and relationships charities are in your area by contacting your local county and councils. Making contact with your local council's health and wellbeing board[3] would be a good place to start in terms of networking with the right people who have a vested interest in supporting your school.

---

2 https://www.gov.uk/government/consultations/transforming-children-and-young-peoples-mental-health-provision-a-green-paper/quick-read-transforming-children-and-young-peoples-mental-health-provision.

3 https://www.kingsfund.org.uk/publications/health-wellbeing-boards-explained.

Cross-curricular interventions
Using yoga and mindfulness as a PSHE or PE cross-curricular intervention

> We want schools to have a whole-school approach that makes talking about feelings, emotions and wellbeing as normal for pupils as talking about their physical bodies. That might include lessons taught as part of the PSHE curriculum, whole-school programmes such as mindfulness that become a normal part of the school day, role play in drama lessons, or offering meditation or yoga sessions. (Edward Timpson MP, Minister for Vulnerable Children and Families, Mindfulness in Schools debate, House of Commons, 6 September 2016)

Anxiety is often cited as a common issue facing young people. Anxiety is a natural response but when it is starting to have a significant impact on the young person's learning, attendance and relationships, then putting into place an intervention which can help them build strategies for coping could be very helpful.

Some schools have investigated the benefits of rolling out yoga and mindfulness as an intervention, which could be introduced in PSHE or PE in six-week rolling blocks, to support students with strategies for combatting building anxiety and panic attacks due to exam pressures. This was effectively carried out at a secondary school in Surrey by yoga teacher Cathy Jones.

Cathy Jones said this of her PSHE yoga sessions:

> I feel the PSHE yoga sessions also offer a safe, quiet place for retreat from the regular school day; time to retreat within themselves and bond with other students in need of peace. The world we live in today is so busy and noisy that taking time out to become still is vital. I believe yoga should be taught in all schools as a coping strategy for life. It builds inner peace and connection, a trust in the universe and practical skills to armour students for life's ups and downs. After all, the main aim of yoga is to yoke the mind and body. Stilling the body and

focusing on the breath brings with it mental stillness, calming the chatter of the monkey brain.

The Instill Conference[4] hosted by TeenYoga in London is a great resource for all interested teachers to attend as it shows teachers how teenagers could benefit from yoga in finding inner strength, building self-esteem and practical strategies for facing inner fears and coping with stress and anxiety.

One way to set up a yoga intervention in your school is to look for a qualified yoga teacher either in your own staff or in your local community and trial running six-week yoga intervention programmes offering it specifically to students showing early signs of challenging emotional and mental wellbeing, particularly anxiety.

There is a lot of misunderstanding about yoga and its links with religious teachings, so it is useful to invite the students (and parents) to a presentation where the history and benefits of yoga are explained.

Of course, participating in any intervention is voluntary and it can work if it takes place during the school's PSHE lesson over the six weeks.

If you can't get hold of a qualified yoga teacher or it is too expensive, you could also roll out Movement and Mindfulness. Moving with mindfulness is simply being more aware of what we are doing, how we are moving – whether it's placing the soles of our feet on the earth, one foot in front of another, holding our pen, feeling our sit bones on a chair or observing sensations when eating a bowl of porridge.

Cathy Jones says: 'It's about uniting the mind with the body; being more aware of the present moment; learning to feel and witness what's going on in our body and around us rather than living in our head and not noticing anything except for incessant mental chatter.'

---

4   www.yogacampus.com/workshops/instill-conference-2018-on-yoga-education-and-well-being-in-schools.

Mindful movement can happen easily in the school setting even without a trained yoga teacher. For example, instead of delivering a PSHE lesson by Powerpoint on Movement and Mindfulness, one teacher took her tutor group out onto the school field. It was a glorious day and, after explaining the purpose, she encouraged them to start walking in any direction alone whilst keeping silent. She suggested they observe each foot fall in front of the other as well as other sensations on a warm November morning. Whilst many did the exercise in groups, there was no doubt by the end of the lesson they were able to share their experiences and what they were more mindful of – warm sun and cool air against the skin was a plus for many. They were appreciative of being in the fresh, open air and experiencing nature.

However Movement and Mindfulness is delivered it is a simple technique to bring one into the present moment and feel . Some schools are using it as a cross-curricular scheme of work in PE. The PE teachers may already have a keen interest in yoga. To enable them to teach yoga-inspired movement classes they could attend a course – Getting started teaching yoga and mindfulness to teens – with TeenYoga (https://teenyoga.com). This course arms the PE teacher with the confidence to take their own yoga practice and merge it with their knowledge of PE, and to devise yoga-inspired movement classes.

In the *Gaia TeenMind* app the mindfulness recordings in the 'My Relaxation' section provide a choice of three audio options covering mindfulness practice of various lengths:

- Grounding and breathing
- Grounding breathing and complete breath
- Physical and breath awareness.

Ms Spencer, a PE teacher in Surrey, used it in her movement and mindfulness classes and has shared an example of a basic format for the PE lesson:

- Using an app on her phone, the students are led through a mindfulness 'body and breath' audio as a starter (five minutes)

- Basic stretches and alignment (five minutes)

- Mindful yoga for beginners – simple movements enabling all students to keep up and understand the breathing technique (25–30 minutes)

- Body scan/individual relaxation time (five minutes).

This cross-curricular intervention was popular with the Year 10 and 11 girls particularly, in the build up to their GCSE exams, and year groups or bands who are disengaged with the PE curriculum.

Mindfulness with students in tutor and PSHE

Mindfulness, as Mark Williams and Danny Penman point out, is a practice. It is a way of being rather than merely a good idea or a clever technique, or a passing fad. The practice of mindfulness has been shown to exert a powerful influence on one's health, wellbeing and happiness.[5]

There are teaching programmes such as those run by the Mindfulness in Schools Project (MISP) which are effective as they start with an eight-week course, then the teacher is encouraged to practise the mindfulness exercises daily. Only once the teachers are practising mindfulness daily, as part of their core practice, are they in a position to sign up to the courses which will guide them on how to deliver programmes for a primary school and secondary school mindfulness in school curriculum. There are a few schools that are delivering this very effectively, such as Aureus Secondary School in Oxfordshire.

I have attended the eight-week foundation course run by MISP and have for a few years practised mindfulness every day

---

5   Williams, M. and Penman, D. (2011) *Mindfulness – A Practical Guide to Finding Peace in a Frantic World.* London: Piatkus Books.

before work and before I come home after work. It helps me get a sense of perspective, of what is important and what is not. It encourages me to focus on my body and breath, which helps enormously with my stress and any anxiety I feel, and it also encourages me to treat myself and others with compassion. It is part of my daily diet and I can 100 per cent attest to the fact that if it were not for my daily practice, I would not have coped with the massive challenges the profession throws at me.

While I would suggest this for all staff, in an ideal situation, it takes time and of course staff need to commit to this lifestyle shift. There is another option, and this is called MindUP.[6] It is a programme based around a mindfulness approach and rooted in neuroscience and breathing as a core practice. It does not require teachers to be practising mindfulness on a daily basis, but it is a research-based programme for young people aged 5–14 that encompasses 15 pre-planned lessons. The programme aims to promote positive wellbeing by using strategies to help pupils learn to enjoy the present moment, be more aware of their own thoughts and feelings and to feel more in control of their behaviour. I have seen it successfully rolled it out with 240 Year 8 students and saw most teachers embrace the core practice with chimes and silent reflection every morning before the start of the school and in their weekly PSHE lessons. In the feedback, the one resounding positive from students and staff was that the one-minute chimed silence – the mindfulness reflection at the start of the day – was gratefully received. Students said it helped them settle and keep them calm. Staff felt it was a great way to draw attention to the students' mental and emotional state, encouraging emotional literacy and, by asking the young people to practise twice a day, was effective in grounding them, bringing them into the moment and allowing them to focus on the lesson which followed.

---

6   https://mindup.org.

If you are a young person suffering from mental wellbeing challenges, having coping strategies like this taught to you, found in yoga and mindfulness, could be invaluable.

After-school, extra-curricular, pop-up-style interventions

A recent campaign from the charity Heads Together provides ten tips for talking to young people about their worries, and these include 'sharing a task' and 'focusing on making something'.[7] This feels very relevant if the school is finding that the young person does not want to sit and talk about their feelings with their teacher, a peer mentor or trained adult mentor, and if the school is battling even to motivate the young person to come to school.

Some schools have trialled extra-curricular, pop-up-style interventions. From the outside, they looked like a 'school pop-up club' or a 'school trip' where students were hanging out with other teens completing creative, non-competitive, extra-curricular tasks. But the reality was that these were structured, time-bonded intervention sessions, with a group of students who were facing mental wellbeing challenges and were on the verge of becoming disengaged with school.

Here are some examples which I have trialled in one school:

- *The Chef's Challenge* – students cooked a different two-course meal each week, set up by chef Mark Lloyd,[8] and then sat down to eat and chat, celebrating each other's efforts in cooking their own dinner.

- *The Bicycle Challenge* – old bicycles were donated and under the guidance of two enthusiastic bike engineer teachers from the design and technology department, students were taught how to remove worn bits and

---

7   https://www.headstogether.org.uk/10-tips-for-talking-to-kids-about-their-worries.

8   www.youtube.com/channel/UCoSZN49AJFSrzLcjRcSKipA.

reassemble with new parts, so they could ride away with a working cycle.

- *The Bush Craft Challenge* – students got to explore bush craft survival skills such as fire lighting, tracking, shelter building, nature art, campfire cooking, outdoor trust games, one-to-one sessions, personal development exercises and mindfulness in nature. Learning outside the classroom in the natural environment has a very positive impact on mental wellbeing and has been superbly documented in the Natural Connections Demonstration Project delivered in South West England by Plymouth University.[9]

The list is endless – just remember to work to the strengths of the teachers and the local community. You could try anything, from gardening and biodiversity clubs to knitting, pottery, art, music, storytelling and being a scientific inventor. Whatever extra-curricular, pop-up-style interventions you choose, try to ensure that they fulfil the objectives, enabling students to:

- know that their input is expected and valued

- finish what they started

- develop a growth mindset and try something out of their comfort zone

- build trust and re-engage their relationship with adults, teachers and peers

- engage in open and sincere communication and sharing

- build resilience by recognising where their sources of help are and their assets.

The good thing about these extra-curricular interventions is that you can use a mixture of adult volunteers, from teaching

---

9   http://publications.naturalengland.org.uk/publication/6636651036540928.

assistants, social workers, counsellors, IT support staff, classroom teachers, and middle and senior leadership staff.

The key to success is that staff are ready to move out of their teaching roles and get on a level playing field with the young people, completing a creative task with them, engaging in discussions and listening with compassion and empathy. In his book, *Inner Story: Understand Your Mind. Change Your World*, Dr Tim O'Brien explains that to show empathy towards others we must first 'flatten' the 'hierarchies of significance' that exist in our mind and understand the world from the perspective of the person we are showing empathy towards. By 'flatten' he simply means that there is a hierarchy of significance in your head and to prevent it being a hierarchy you flatten it so that nothing is more significant than anything else – thus making the teacher less judgemental. Students feel deeply appreciative when they are simply understood – not evaluated, not judged – from their own point of view, not the teacher's.[10]

The results

In the examples trialled in my school, the first few sessions were about building trust and getting involved in the activities but as the sessions progressed the young people started to relax and, in the process, personal information was revealed about their home life, their fears and their struggles. This enabled the adults to build a detailed picture of their physical health, attitude to school, friendships, personal confidence, family relationships, values and communication skills. Some students were highlighted by the adults facilitating the intervention as 'troubled' and a cause for real concern about their general emotional wellbeing. Some of the observations were new and some only served to enforce what we as a school were already finding; for example, there were issues with personal safety, sexual identity, respect and relationships, family relationships

---

10 O'Brien, T. (2015) *Inner Story: Understand Your Mind. Change Your World.* CreateSpace.

and relationship with food. Referrals were then put in place for further intervention relevant to these needs.

In the feedback from the 40 students who took part, all students reported a marked improvement in self-worth, feeling useful, feeling more relaxed, being able to make clearer decisions and experiencing a definite enjoyment of the sessions.

It wasn't just the students who gave positive feedback; staff were impressed too:

- This was the first time I have ever encountered Tobias apart from dealing with behaviour issues (I've never taught him) and he seemed like a different person.

- Tom began the programme by making it obvious that he did not want to be there. However, by week two, I saw a very different young person. He became more involved and tried more things. He made more eye contact and began to engage in conversation with staff. He also integrated more into the group. He showed an ability to stay on task over a considerable length of time. He took instruction well, applying it to his learning. He became generally easy to have around.

- Sarah has significantly fewer behaviour points in school since she started and has put her name forward for a student leadership role.

- Making food is a great leveller as all adults and students in the room were learning something new together. This allowed for humour, trust and private conversations to flow.

The real value in this pop-up club intervention idea is to allow the students to have some real face-to-face support with an empathetic adult while doing a creative activity. Because I did not have to 'teach' or 'manage' a class, I was able to take time out to really listen, walk and talk, sit and laugh, ask for help. Connections were made. The healing process had begun.

It needs to be noted that there is no quick fix. The mental wellbeing challenge does not go away, nor does the adversity facing them in their personal lives *but* what does change is their trust relationship with the teachers; how they view themselves. And they gain a greater awareness of their strengths and the resources available to them, and therefore their resilience improves.

Finally, encouraging young people to get involved in after-school clubs and school schemes is a guaranteed way to help the young people feel a sense of connectedness, which is a recognised protective factor for mental wellbeing. It gives them resources in terms of the relationships they develop with peers and adults – these may well be the relationships they turn to for support later in their lives. The involvement also helps them develop self-value, not to mention looking great on their CV as a point of interest about their character.

However, the problem is many of our young people showing challenging signs with mental health are not signed up to be part of extra-curricular clubs. For many it may be because of cost. Having access to a balanced curriculum is rapidly becoming the privilege of the middle class and those that can afford it. It may be because they are a young carer and are expected to be at home to complete tasks; sometimes it is because of the pressure of being a failure and they have low resilience; or they simply have not received support and encouragement from home.

I am not saying that being part of a club and hanging out with other students is a panacea for all early mental wellbeing ills, but we have found that inviting groups of students with mental wellbeing challenges to be part of a creative, practical pop-up club, in a controlled environment with empathetic adults, is vital to re-engaging them and making them feel valued. This could be key to effective early mental wellbeing intervention strategies, especially when in-class interventions have failed.

15

Work with Parents

KEY POINTS

* The role of the parents is essential in engaging in mental wellbeing conversations and promoting lifestyle choices that encourage positive mental wellbeing.

* There are many ways in which we can engage parents from creative campaign work, awareness-raising letters home, offering tea and chat sessions and using local community charities to support and involve them in the proposed interventions and strategies.

* We need to encourage families to see mental wellbeing as the development of mental wealth.

The success of any school mental wellbeing and wellbeing programme is dependent on five main factors:

1. The school providing curriculum time and space to talk about mental wellbeing and to develop a culture of promoting positive mental wellbeing.

2. The individual student's level of engagement and seeing the relevance of taking part.

3. The role of the staff and their own mental wellbeing.

4. The role of the parents in engaging in mental wellbeing conversations and promoting lifestyle choices that encourage positive mental wellbeing.

5. The extent to which the local community gets involved and the school engages the services of local external agencies.

It is widely regarded that parents and schools form a 50/50 partnership in bringing up and educating children and that if both parties work together then there is consistency for the child, and the life skills we are teaching are more likely to be accepted.

There are many ways in which we can engage parents, all of which are analysed in greater detail in this chapter:

- To raise awareness of mental wellbeing and its importance for the whole family unit.

- To destigmatise mental health and offer a space to hold a constructive conversation with the parent and ask effective questions about the mental wellbeing challenge their child might be facing.

- To offer a space to share and reflect on their own mental wellbeing and resilience.

- To offer a platform for parents to make and role-model positive lifestyle choices.

- To offer routes for having a say on interventions and feedback.

To raise awareness of mental wellbeing and its importance for the whole family unit

What resources have you provided/signposted for parents to better address mental wellbeing and destigmatise it? Where and when can these resources be accessed?

I would encourage schools to have a tab on their website or an app, showing where the details are for a concerned parent. I also encourage regular information drops. For example, I sent out three letters to parents and guardians talking about the wellbeing zone and what is on offer, what mental wellbeing is and how parents can seek support, and encouraging parents to get behind the #familyMH5aday campaign (more on this later).

Many schools have created a mental wellbeing advice list of what the parents should or should not be letting the children do, with a strong emphasis on sleep, digital screen time and online behaviour. This is all very relevant. But what about the parents?

- If parents spend much of their day with their faces buried in their 'screen time' how is this impacting on their 'real-time' family relationships?

- If parents are constantly 'working' and have a poor work–life balance, what subliminal message is this sending out about the value we attach to having a quality standard of life?

- If parents have stopped reading, learning and trying new things, what message is this sending out about the value of play, learning and having a growth mindset?

- If parents are prioritising everything that is material and don't give and volunteer time for others, what is this saying about being aware of the needs of others?

- If parents have stopped relating and engaging in conversation with their children, how can they expect the children to have the confidence to approach them when they need to talk or to develop and sustain mutually satisfying relationships?

- If parents are suffering from a mental health illness or challenge and are not talking about it or seeking help, how is this reinforcing the stigma at home?

For a student wellbeing programme to work, we need to connect parents with the work we are doing in school; we need parents role-modelling from the top – pushing for an environment at home which nurtures positive mental wellbeing. We need to encourage families to see mental wellbeing as the development of 'mental wealth.'

But let's be honest here, parents are the hardest audience to reach. Schools have limited contact, and it is difficult to lecture parents, as it may be perceived as interfering with their parenting, and they may have many different attitudes to wellbeing and mental health.

The #familyMH5aday campaign is simple and easy to follow, adaptable, light hearted, positive and fun. But it has real impact and enables parents to model behaviours, which is crucial to reinforcing the work of the school. It's about getting the parents, carers, grandparents and siblings to come together, engage in positive interaction with each other and take part in a range of activities which encourage real-time connection with each other and the world around them before digital time connection takes over. I launched #familyMH5aday campaign in my own family unit and through my school and it involves embracing five lifestyle concepts which promote positive mental wellbeing. I call it living the GREAT values:

G – Give

R – Relate

E – Energise

A – Awareness

T – Try something new.

You can find out more about the #familyMH5aday campaign in a TEDx talk[1] I did with my daughter. Its title is 'How to strengthen family relationships by Rosie and Clare Erasmus'. Appendix 5

---

1   www.youtube.com/watch?v=c5tuaUFyQrE.

at the end of this book has some suggestions for activities for parents and students around the #familyMH5aday theme.

To hold a constructive conversation with the parent and ask effective questions about the mental wellbeing challenge their child might be facing

This is a general guide for teachers on how to conduct that conversation with a parent which will help the teacher build a picture of the student and identity possible appropriate interventions. Remember, our role is not to diagnose but to be pre-emptive and proactive. The questions you ask should reflect this.

- Try and capture a picture of what the child enjoys and what they look forward to.

- Ask the parent to share any areas of concern about their child, such as changes in diet, friendship circles, social life, language, interests, obsessions.

- Ascertain when the child is not showing these areas of concern. Where do they appear most at ease?

- What do they think is bringing on the young person's difficulties?

- How concerned do they think the child is?

- How long has it been going on for? When did it start?

- Are there any strategies that have worked?

- Are there any agencies involved? What are they suggesting? Who could the parents try to get involved?

- What would the parents like to happen?

- Talk about what resources the school might have to put interventions in place.

- End the conversation with follow-up strategies and possible short-term interventions.

It is vital parents recognise that schools are not able to offer counselling services unless they have a resident counsellor. Stress to your teachers *never* to offer a diagnosis and services you cannot guarantee but instead to offer pre-emptive and proactive support with available resources.

To offer a space to share and reflect on their own mental wellbeing and resilience

In one school, they also teamed up with a local external agency, East to West,[2] to host tea and chat sessions once each half term, inviting parents to an event called Parent Headspace. The charity was able to offer home support and speakers and advice for the parents and it was an important link in breaking down barriers between school and the family unit, ensuring all felt supported.

I have also had the pleasure of working with an external company called The Resilience Doughnut,[3] (see Chapter 5) which visits schools to deliver a workshop on raising resilient children and teenagers. This is all about how The Resilience Doughnut can help parents discover ways to support their children as they grow and change, so that they can face the inevitable difficulties that life sometimes brings. It shows parents the areas of strength that are already working well in their child's life and gives ideas about how to use these strengths to enhance resilience further. Parents are raising their children in isolation, and The Resilience Doughnut empowers parents to draw on all the other resources that are available to them and combines these positive strategies to support them in raising their children. Through the workshop, the focus is shifted from child managing to child raising. In the process, parents develop a range of conversational skills which can be used in everyday

2   www.easttowest.org.uk.
3   https://www.resiliencedoughnutuk.com.

situations and during times of challenge to enhance their child's sense of agency (I can), awareness of social resources (I have) and view of themselves and their inner strengths (I am).

To offer a platform for parents to make and role-model positive lifestyle choices

This was an exciting venture where one school asked parents to come forward and volunteer to be parent wellbeing ambassadors.

They were part of a pilot where they got to chart its direction and how it would function as an online community. Some of our parent wellbeing ambassadors tweeted as @wellbeingparent, offering advice on and promoting:

- de-stressing your home at exam times
- five a day for good mental wellbeing in your home
- work–life balance
- positive parenting
- support for parents
- classes and events which could be good for whole family/ parent/teen wellbeing
- yoga and activity and leisure groups.

The parent wellbeing ambassadors were also a good group to use for consulting on matters where the school wished to engage with parents. They were positive and realistic in their feedback and advice.

To offer routes for having a say on interventions and feedback

When a young person is identified as needing support and they have gone through the initial interventions with a teacher and middle leader pastoral managers, it might be clear that this young person needs to be quickly escalated for a staff referral for further intervention. The young person should be triaged at this point and their priority need identified. The question you should ask is: Is it a learning need, a pastoral need or an SEN need? Once the young person has been flagged up it is vital that an individual mental wellbeing care plan is set up and the parents are contacted and notified about the intervention taking place. It could take place across a period of six weeks in the form of a one-to-one session, a workshop, groupwork or a series of sessions with a specialist external agency – either way, it is vital that the parents are fully informed, their consent is sought, and they are brought on board in terms of their possible role and support at home.

16

Whole-School Campaigns

KEY POINTS

* Focusing on mental wellbeing is more than just an anti-bullying day or a health and wellbeing week, but they're a good place to start.

* Establishing shared values in a school is an excellent way to galvanise the school round a joint purpose.

* The GREAT values is a challenge to make small lifestyle changes to embrace a healthier mental wellbeing lifestyle.

No one doubts the importance of numeracy and literacy for the fast-changing world which lies ahead of our young people. But if students are not emotionally literate about their own mental wellbeing; given target-specific support with mental wellbeing challenges; given in-depth exploration about what is a positive and negative relationship and how to conduct yourself in real time and digital time; taught strategies for dealing with anxiety and stress; taught to recognise that eating disorders and substance misuse are all forms of self-harm...then we are failing them. We will be churning out a shell that has been spoonfed to enable them to pass an exam...but what about passing the resilience test called *life*? We need to change the narrative from only focusing on mental health illnesses and instead be focusing in our core curriculum on what it means and takes to be a 'well being'. In the YoungMinds *Wise Up: Prioritising Wellbeing in Schools* publication, Chief Executive Sarah Brennan says:

> Students need education to include how to understand and look after their mental wellbeing – just like we learn how to look after our physical health. By shifting the focus to preventing mental wellbeing problems and building resilience we can do so much to improve the lives of so many. Good wellbeing on leaving school has a much greater impact on life outcomes than exam success.[1]

Our youth are having to be more grown up than ever before. They are being presented with scenarios online that they are often not emotionally fully prepared for but are expected to make discerning choices about how to engage or not engage. The YoungMinds report states that:

> 90% of school leaders have reported an increase in the number of students experiencing anxiety or stress over the last five years.

> 80% of young people saying that exam pressure has significantly impacted on their mental wellbeing.

> The number of young people attending A&E because of a psychiatric condition more than doubled between 2010/11 and 2014/15.

> The number of young people calling Childline about mental wellbeing problems has risen by 36% in the last four years.

> Rates of depression and anxiety in teenagers have increased by 70% in the past 25 years.[2]

---

1   YoungMinds (2017) *Wise Up: Prioritising Wellbeing in Schools.* YoungMinds, p.2.
2   YoungMinds (2017) *Wise Up: Prioritising Wellbeing in Schools.* YoungMinds.

They are also witnessing adults working longer hours, showing clear signs of stress and often shocking examples of work–life balance. Time spent with the family communicating is now only achieved through a concerted disciplined effort from everyone to 'down tool' digital devices and to connect with each other.

In the past, youth mental health and wellbeing has often been a Cinderella subject in schools, only addressed in the occasional PSHE lesson. Schools need to take this seriously and embed this support in their value systems and broad curriculum. I am delighted that the latest Green Paper[3] pledged that from 2020 schools will be required to deliver compulsory health education in the curriculum, and mental resilience and wellbeing will form a key element of this new subject.

There are many ways we can tackle delivering this aspect in the curriculum. The first thing you can do is highlight all the big national events relevant to your school community which you can encourage your school to get behind. Look for campaigns that will really resonate with the need in your school – for example, if stress is high among teachers and students, perhaps a stress awareness week might be prudent. If suicide ideation is prevalent, then World Suicide Prevention Day would be valuable for your school to explore. By doing this, your school will be sending a clear message that mental wellbeing is a concept we value the most in preparing for *life*.

To help you select what could be your school focus for each year, here is a list of events, adapted from the calendar on the Time To change website.[4]

---

3   *Government Response to the Consultation on 'Transforming Children and Young People's Mental Health Provision: A Green Paper' and Next Steps* (2018) London: Department for Education.

4   www.time-to-change.org.uk/get-involved/tackle-stigma-workplace/make-impact-your-workplace/mental-health-calendar.

February
Time to Talk Day
The aim of this day is to get as many people as possible across England talking about mental wellbeing. By joining together on one day, we can break the silence that often surrounds mental wellbeing, and show that talking about this once-taboo issue doesn't need to be difficult.
Eating Disorders Awareness Week
This is an international awareness event, fighting the myths and misunderstandings that surround eating disorders.   Find out more: www.b-eat.co.uk/support-us/eating-disorder-awareness-week
Children's Mental Wellbeing Week
This campaign hopes to raise awareness of the benefits of getting children support at the earliest possible opportunity, and to encourage parents to talk openly with children about their feelings and getting help.   Find out more: www.place2be.org.uk
March
University Mental Wellbeing Day
This is an annual event to promote the mental wellbeing of those who live and work in higher education settings. The initiative was started by the University Mental Wellbeing Advisers Network in 2012 and is supported by Student Minds and members of the Alliance for Student-Led Wellbeing.   Find out more: www.studentminds.org.uk
World Bipolar Day
The purpose of the day is to raise awareness of bipolar disorders and to improve sensitivity towards the illness. It is promoted by the International Bipolar Foundation and partners.   Find out more: www.ibpf.org/blog/world-bipolar-day
April
Stress Awareness Month
Find out more: www.awarenessdays.com/awareness-days-calendar/stress-awareness-month-2018
May
Mental Wellbeing Awareness Week
Raising awareness of mental wellbeing and wellbeing every year, promoted by the Mental Wellbeing Foundation.   Find out more: www.mentalhealth.org.uk/our-work/mentalhealthawarenessweek

June
Volunteers' Week
This is an annual event run by the National Council of Voluntary Organisations to celebrate volunteers and volunteering. Find out more: http://volunteersweek.org/about
September
World Suicide Prevention Day – 10 September
Organised by the International Association for Suicide Prevention and the World Health Organisation, the purpose of the day is to promote worldwide commitment and action to prevent suicides. Find out more: www.iasp.info/wspd/index.php
October
World Mental Health Day
This falls on 10 October every year, with the overall objective of raising awareness of mental health issues around the world and mobilising efforts in support of mental health. The day provides an opportunity for all stakeholders working on mental health issues to talk about their work, and what more needs to be done to make mental health care a reality for people worldwide. Find out more: www.who.int/mental_health
November
National Stress Awareness Day
Normally held on the first Wednesday of November each year, this day is promoted by the International Stress Management Association. The purpose of the day is to raise awareness of the effects of psychological distress in the workplace and of the many coping strategies and sources of help available to address it. Find out more: www.isma.org.uk/about-national-stressawareness-day-nsad
Anti-Bullying Week
This is held during a week in middle of November and often is accompanied by a theme. Good websites to refer to are www.anti-bullyingalliance.org.uk, and https://www.antibullyingpro.com and https://diana-award.org.uk.

We need to make sure that the culture of the school is also changed from within – focusing on mental wellbeing is *more* than just an anti-bullying day or a health and wellbeing week.

I once asked a headteacher what their school's values were and I was given a handful of academic and career-orientated aspirational values. I explained these weren't holistic values – values which would help the young person build a strong sense of self and sense of community.

I am a strong believer that establishing shared values in a school is an excellent way to galvanise a school around a joint purpose. A great example is the work taking place in values-based education schools. These values are collated from all key stakeholders in a school's community and then a different one is championed each month in all lessons and across the school day. Shared values devised at grassroots will bind a community together and be far more effective than top-down enforced 'rules'. More can be found about the work of Dr Neil Hawkes and values-based education at www.valuesbasededucation.com.

Becoming a values-based school really does need direction and commitment from the top – from the leadership and governing body team. For many schools, this seems too big a leap, which means we need to introduce this culture in different ways – through a series of carefully selected whole-school campaigns.

Case study: Embracing the GREAT values

Having researched the host of wellbeing sites I found that they all shared how our health and happiness can be boosted by doing certain things on a day-to-day basis. Based on this principle, the acronym GREAT values was conceived.

G – Give

R – Relate

E – Energise

A – Awareness

T – Try something new

The idea is that we can all make small lifestyle changes to create a culture of wellbeing, and this led to the #familyMH5aday, GREAT values campaign being adopted at my school.

The challenge was how to encourage an entire year group of young teenagers to embrace this campaign. The first step was to build up a support team, and here you need to turn to your proactive wellbeing staff team who you can rely on for support and, of course, your student wellbeing ambassadors.

We recognised that a key factor is the parents – they also need to sign up to a shared value system which embraces a positive mental wellbeing lifestyle.

We sent out request via Twitter and parent mail for volunteers to come forward and be the school's parent wellbeing ambassadors. A very generous, enthusiastic group of parents volunteered and I was able to bounce ideas off them and to generate new ideas for the school concept of #familyMH5aday.

Christmas is a good season to launch the GREAT campaign as it dovetails with many of the religious values of giving to others and being grateful, reflecting on the past and resting and re-energising for the new year.

The concept is simple.

Each year group is given a list of GREAT activities to do at home in the build up to Christmas with family and friends. In exchange for getting one activity signed off they are awarded points (this works well when run in conjunction with an active inter-house competition system).

Thanks to the enormous help of the wellbeing student and parent ambassadors I worked with, activity sheets were created (see Appendix 5).

So, what was the take up?

The successful groups were the ones where the teachers joined in, where students incorporated the values into their everyday connections with each other. One group was amazing as they launched breakfast and lunchtime clubs together and now have a very close bond with each other and their teacher. If the adults were leading by example the young people enthusiastically joined in. That is the key. That is why there is a sheet for the parents too – it gives them an opportunity to sign off activities and embrace their ability to commit to the GREAT values.

The #familyMHaday campaign is more than just a challenge to make small lifestyle changes to embrace a healthier mental wellbeing lifestyle – it is a plea for parents to check the level of 'disconnection' taking place under the family roof and to revive 'real-time' connections with family members.

17

Share Best Practice

KEY POINTS

* Keep up to date by networking on social media platforms like Twitter to read what the experts are saying.

* Read blogs written by other mental health practitioners in schools.

* Blog about your journey and share your trials and tribulations. We are breaking new ground here and need to share as much information as possible.

When I was appointed the lead on mental health and wellbeing, the first thing I looked for was training.

In those days, I was limited to a few key conferences led by mental wellbeing experts where the focus was particularly for the safeguarding or SENCO lead and there were few opportunities to share best practice for the teacher.

It felt quite a lonely existence and I was on a real search for practical strategies suited for a school environment and to share best practice with other educators.

I am delighted to say things have changed considerably over the last four years. Here are my top suggestions on how to get connected with people and organisations who can share best practice and ideas for you and your school:

1. Get yourself onto Twitter and follow some key wellbeing warriors in education. There are some fabulous people I can connect you with. If you follow me on @cerasmusteach I will quickly connect you with people who can help you in your area. To get started, try following the Charlie Waller Memorial Trust, Heads Together, YoungMinds and the Anna Freud National Centre for Children and Families. These key players will be posting information all the time, with subject matter relevant to educators working with children in the area of mental health.

2. Contact the Charlie Waller Memorial Trust for cost-effective training in schools on a host of topics from eating disorders, self-harm, suicide ideation, to spotting the signs and holding the first conversation. Its YouTube site hosts an enormous range of films to guide any teacher and lead on mental wellbeing from basic definitions to continuing professional development on how to spot the signs.

3. To stay up to date with the latest evidence-based health and social care research, the Mental Health Elf (@Mental_Elf) is an incredibly helpful section of the National Elf Service website. I have found the blogs posted on mental wellbeing incredibly useful. You can find more at www.nationalelfservice.net.

4. Take a look at Dr Pooky Knightsmith's helpful webinars and YouTube short videos about supporting youth mental wellbeing. You can find these on her website (www.pookyknightsmith.com/videos). Also on her YouTube channel, you can find wellbeing chat, tips and information. I have found these really helpful when I have needed to deliver tailor-made in-service training in our school or to help a teacher who requests additional reading material on a specific topic.

5. Visit Heads Together Mentally Healthy Schools (www. mentallyhealthyschools.org.uk), which brings together quality-assured information, advice and resources to help primary schools understand and promote children's mental health and wellbeing. This website offers hundreds of teaching resources including assembly plans and PSHE resources on mental wellbeing.

6. Visit Nip in the Bud's site (https://nipinthebud.org) for some excellent videos exploring the topics of mental ill-health. Nip in the Bud was set up to encourage awareness about mental health disorders in young children. Its films illustrate the behaviours common in different conditions in children, along with explanations and information on how to follow up and get help. The films are accompanied by downloadable fact sheets explaining the symptoms to look out for to spot early signs of distress which may require further monitoring.

7. Visit MindEd (www.minded.org.uk). It is designed to meet your needs whether you are completely new to children and young people's mental health or are very experienced. It covers universal care through to specialist content. In addition, you will be introduced to MindEd for Families. These sessions were co-created with parents specifically to support parents and carers.

8. Visit Dr Sue Roffey's Growing Great Schools Worldwide website (https://growinggreatschoolsworldwide.com), which offers a range of services from talks, workshops, research and consultancy. Sue has written some powerful books, which I recommend you read.

9. Visit SchoolWell (http://schoolwell.co.uk), a great resource for staff workload and mental wellbeing. There is directory of wellbeing resources for school staff.

10. See The Resilience Doughnut website (www.resiliencedoughnutuk.com), another important resource for resilience training with staff, students and parents.

11. Join the Chartered College of Teaching and link up with its thematic networks. It is currently running small cell group sessions for supporting youth mental wellbeing in a school setting and you will be able to attend a local TeachMeet for your area.

12. Follow the Carnegie Centre of Excellence for Mental Health in Schools based at Leeds Beckett University (http://leedsbeckett.ac.uk/schoolMH). It runs excellent courses for mental wellbeing leads and has a mental health quality mark for schools to follow. It tweets under @SchoolMHealth and can be contacted by email on schoolmh@leedsbeckett.ac.uk.

13. If you get a chance, visit The Aureus School in Oxfordshire and see how it has managed to embed a culture across the school curriculum of supporting youth mental wellbeing and wellbeing. You can follow the trail blazer head Hannah Wilson on Twitter. This school is becoming a regular feature for hosting youth mental wellbeing focused TeachMeets.

14. Follow the PSHE association (www.pshe-association.org.uk) for PSHE advice and how it can be woven into the curriculum.

15. Finally, blog about your journey. Share your trials and tribulations. The web space is a wonderful way to connect with educators on a global scale and to share best practice. When it comes to supporting youth mental wellbeing and wellbeing, it is important we enable all classroom practitioners with practical strategies for all levels and environments.

Lead on Mental Wellbeing: Roles and Responsibilities

The UK government's *Transforming Children and Young People's Mental Health Provision: A Green Paper* stated:

> We want every school and college to have a designated lead in mental health by 2025. The designated lead will be a trained member of staff who is responsible for the school's approach to mental health.
>
> This designated lead will:
>
> - oversee the help the school gives to pupils with mental health problems
>
> - help staff to spot pupils who show signs of mental health problems
>
> - offer advice to staff about mental health
>
> - refer children to specialist services if they need to.

An overview of how you could lead what the role entails
Student wellbeing

- Gather qualitative data: run extensive focus group sessions with 10 per cent of the student population and possibly coordinate with external research agencies.

- Gather quantitative data: create and run student wellbeing questionnaire using Survey Monkey (base questionnaire questions on main issues raised in initial focus groups).

- Present research to governors.

- Work with staff on existing student wellbeing initiatives. Contact county healthy schools status recognition programmes. Engage all key stakeholders in what makes a healthy school.

- Set up wellbeing safe spaces for students.

- Work with tutor groups in running a mental wellbeing curriculum which raises mental and emotional literacy, and sharing strategies for support.

Coordinate internal tracking system

- Ensure all visits are logged and intervention is tracked (use SIMS/Provision Mapping in intervention section so students' details are all saved in one place, hard copies for triage, assessment, time bonded intervention, impact).

- Design a flow chart for reporting and referrals and intervention stages for mental health and wellbeing to ensure safeguarding.

- Ensure communication happens with the special educational needs coordinator and the designated safeguarding lead so that everyone has access to key information.

Note: If a student is already with CAMHS or working with a specialist service, ensure thorough communication is happening to prevent overwhelming the student with too much support or conflicting therapies/interventions.

Training staff and staff wellbeing

Ask your headteacher for an opportunity to have at least one in-service training day a year focused on mental wellbeing. You can either get outside speakers in or you can lead it yourself. Topics can range from teacher wellbeing, handling stress, mindfulness, spotting the signs, holding that first conversation to topic specific in-service training like self-harm, suicide ideation, eating disorders, anxiety and panic attacks.

- Organise and lead whole staff in-service training on:

    - signs to look out for or/and specific mental health challenges facing the young person in the school

    - how to hold that first conversation with students

    - working with parents.

- Deliver training to staff on how the flow chart and referral procedures for a student work.

- Work with senior leadership team and create a staff wellbeing action group responding to staff wellbeing concerns.

- Help draft staff a questionnaire or hold focus groups to assess mental wellbeing in the workplace.

- Help coordinate with the senior leadership team feedback sessions and a 'You said. We did' response.

- Encourage others and help initiate fun staff wellbeing programmes. For example, biggest loser (weight loss), yoga, boot camps, mindfulness training, slow days, socials, stop the clocks. (*Note:* The above could be done solely by a member of senior leadership team but it is advisable to have the lead on mental wellbeing on board in an advisory capacity to ensure that the staff voice is properly represented and heard.)

- Ensure staff engagement with student voice and wellbeing policies and reporting procedures.

- Run staff twilight training sessions, working on a staff coordinated response to the student voice (from primary research conducted) and then coordinate the results.

Note: Don't try and use the whole staff body if it is a very big school. Instead, create a wellbeing think tank – invite key staff to join and ensure representation from all areas, including academic progress, PSHE, canteen, PE and extra-curricular, the arts, SEN and mental health.

Recruit and train wellbeing ambassadors and adult mentors

Note: This is one area where you don't cut corners. Train the student wellbeing ambassadors and their adult wellbeing ambassadors properly.

- Ensure key staff are trained as mental health first aiders.

- Ensure wellbeing ambassadors are trained in listening skills, safeguarding and signposting.

Coordinate cross-curricular digital resources

- Establish a presence on the school website with advice for parents and young people.

- Liaise with Gaia Technologies in the building of a customised *My TeenMind* app.

Coordinate a health and wellbeing week and a mental health day

- Engage outside local community agencies.

- Design an activity programme.

- In advance, deliver a detailed presentation to the following to ensure everyone has joined-up thinking and can be proactive:

  - lead teachers

  - teachers

  - all student year groups and houses

  - governors.

Coordinate delivery of mental health and wellbeing lessons in PSHE

- Work with the head of PSHE in training staff on how to deliver effective PSHE which covers lessons addressing mental health, resilience and being proactive about adopting positive lifestyle choices to support personal mental wellbeing.

- Work with the head of PSHE in creating mental health and wellbeing lessons which are relevant and engaging (see PSHE association website, Heads Together, YoungMinds, Time to Talk etc.).

Write a mental heath and wellbeing guidance document

- Ensure that staff and parents can clearly see who the contact people are and what are the internal referral procedures.

When in doubt, ask yourself these questions

- Who is leading the initiatives, and do they have the mandate to implement change?

- What policies do you have which cover mental health and wellbeing? Are they effective in delivering support and for whom?

- Where do you have mental health lessons in the curriculum and what outside agencies are you using to facilitate greater understanding?

- How are you encouraging your students to learn and what language are you using in teaching?

- What student and staff initiatives are embedded in your school culture, your ethos and your environment which clearly point to supporting and promoting mental health and wellbeing?

- What physical spaces have you allocated for mental wellbeing support work? Is this part of SEN or separate? Does it matter?

- What support structures are there in place for a student to:

  - identify and research these mental wellbeing challenges

  - seek support?

- How have you signposted these physical spaces for your students, so that they know:

  - where to go to seek support

  - when they can visit

  - who is available for them to see?

- What evidence do you have that you have given students a voice on their mental health and wellbeing?

- What role do you see your students playing in supporting youth mental wellbeing? What additional skills do the students need?

- What are some unique risk factors young students face for developing mental wellbeing problems?

- What mental wellbeing support services do you offer in your school and in your community?

- Who do you have to be adult mentors or counsellors? What continuing professional development training have they had, or can they have?

- What intervention programmes have you in place for pre-emptive support?

- What opportunities have you tapped into or can you tap into for cross-curricular mental wellbeing work?

- What evidence do you have that *all* staff have been given opportunities for continuing professional development with mental health teaching and with supporting their own mental health and wellbeing?

- What role do you see your teachers and school staff playing in supporting students' mental wellbeing? What do you need to enable this to happen?

- How can your school community be more supportive of each other's mental wellbeing at school?

- How are your parents/carers and local community engaged with mental health and wellbeing initiatives?

- What resources have you provided/signposted for parents, teachers and young people to use to better address mental wellbeing?

- How are you assessing and tracking achievement and what do you consider achievement?

- What whole-school campaigns have you been running to highlight mental wellbeing and wellbeing? What whole-school campaigns can you run?

- What are the 'areas of resistance' facing you in prioritising and implementing a mental wellbeing programme? What are your options in getting around this?

Example of a Mental Health and Wellbeing Policy

A well-developed and implemented policy can prevent students from falling through the gaps. How to write a Mental Health and Wellbeing Policing for Schools and Colleges is a freely downloadable guide and template found on the Charlie Waller Memorial Trust website. It has been designed to help schools develop policies and procedures which will empower staff to spot and support students in need of help and to follow appropriate referral pathways and procedures. This guidance was written by Dr Pooky Knightsmith as part of her work with the Charlie Waller Memorial Trust.

Please visit the following site to download the full template available to you: www.cwmt.org.uk/mental-health-policy.

Example of a Generic Staff Wellbeing Survey

This workplace would like to improve the health and wellbeing of its staff by ensuring a healthier, safer and supportive working environment.

In order to do this, we would like staff to complete this questionnaire so that we can identify the key issues and develop an action plan around these.

Please fill it in – this is your chance to have a real say and make positive changes within the school.

All your answers and comments will remain completely confidential. The survey contains sets of statements that seek to investigate issues relating to:

- the demands of your work

- the amount of control you have over your work

- the amount of support you receive at work

- the working relationships you have with colleagues

- your experience of pupil behaviour

- your role at work

- your involvement in workplace changes

- the pressures and stresses associated with your work.

It is not necessary for you to answer questions in sections that are of no interest to you.

What is your role in school?:

Support staff – admin/premises

Support staff – learning

Class teacher

Middle leader

Senior leader

Please tick the response which most applies to you, for the following statements:	True	Mostly true	Sometimes true	Seldom true	Not true	NA
Demands						
I cope well with the demands placed on me at work						
The workload arising from the planning and assessment of students' work is acceptable						
I feel that my skills are well matched to the work I am asked to undertake						
I feel able to raise with those who manage me any concerns I may have about the demands made of me at work						
Comments:						
Role						
I feel that my performance management objectives are achievable						

cont.

I feel able to raise with those who manage me any concerns I may have about my role within the workplace						

Comments:

Support						
I feel supported in the work I do						
I feel our team works well together and we support each other						

Comments:

Change						
I am consulted about proposed changes that affect me						
My views about proposed changes that affect me are listened to						
I am told why changes in the workplace are being considered						
I cope well with the pace of organisational change within the workplace						
I cope well with the pace of curriculum changes						
Changes affecting me are accompanied by appropriate support and training						

Comments:

Control						
I am in control of the way in which I plan and organise my work						
I am encouraged to use my professional judgement						
I am able to influence my future career development						
I have been adequately trained for the work that I am asked to undertake						
I have access to the curriculum resources I need to deliver the results expected of me						
I have access to the classroom support needed to deliver the results expected of me						
Comments:						

Relationships						
I can rely on the cooperation of colleagues where delivery of my work requires their assistance						
Arrangements to observe my lessons are acceptable						
I receive constructive feedback from those who observe my work						
I have a positive working relationship with colleagues						
Student behaviour is acceptable						
I am encouraged to report incidents of unacceptable student behaviour						
Comments:						

cont.

Health						
I consider that I have a healthy lifestyle						
I would like to improve my health						
I make use of the sports facilities in school						
I have sufficient time to relax during the working day						
I have, during the last six months, suffered from work-related stress						
I have, during the last six months, taken time off work due to work-related stress						
Comments:						

Please comment on any other area of your work that has not been covered above:

_____

_____

_____

_____

_____

_____

Please give ideas or make practical suggestions which would help improve the health and wellbeing of our staff:

_____

_____

_____

_____

_____

Appendix 4

Generic Student Mental Wellbeing Internal Referral Form

This form is to be filled in only after first stage interventions have already taken place with: Stage 1: Form Tutor (two weeks minimum intervention).

If no improvement is noted with the student, *then* referral is made.

Important points to consider:

- *It is not our place to diagnose* the student with any condition. It is our place to be pre-emptive and proactive. CAMHS and GP diagnose.

- *Ensure all forms* are kept in student's file for evidence in case a referral needs to be made.

- *We are not a counselling service*; instead, we offer non-directive therapy (listening with empathy, offering support and signposting, helping the student to problem solve for themselves). Where possible we bring in expert agencies with specialised skills.

Generic Student Mental Wellbeing Internal Referral Form

Date:

Referred by:

Student name:

SEN: P.P: Y/N   On C.P. Reg: Y/N   Y/Carer: Y/N

FSM: Y/N

Attendance %:   Behaviour points:

Achievement points:

Is parent/carer aware of referral?

Have you had a conversation with parent/carer?

What interventions have been implemented so far (please highlight)?

Tutee mentoring

Tutor report

Pop-in lunchtime spaces in #wellbeingsquare

Reason for referral/issues/concerns:

- Anger
- Bully/Bullying
- Bereavement
- Family
- Obsessive-compulsive behaviour
- Self-harm
- Young carer
- Anxiety
- Depression

- Eating disorders
- Friendships
- Self-esteem (low)
- Substance misuse
- Other
- Please specify_____

Do you think they would benefit from:

- group-work intervention
- one to one
- same-sex mentor
- extra-curricular styled intervention?
- Any other relevant information_____

Individual Mental Wellbeing Care Plan

Has the teacher or head of year had a conversation with the parent?

What was the outcome?

Is the young person known to CAMHS?

Is the young person known to any other counselling service?

If so which agency?

Are they known to our designated safeguarding lead?

Are they known to the SENCO?

What intervention would suit them best?

Who or what agency would be best to mentor the student?

What does the young person want from this referral?

What type of six-week intervention is to be put in place?

Appendix 5

Examples of #familyMH5aday activities

Want to have positive mental wellbeing as a family? Embrace these GREAT values. Student activities #familyMH5aday					
Week	G = GIVE	R = RELATE	E = ENERGISE	A = AWARENESS	T = TRY SOMETHING NEW
1	Hug a friend/ buddy/family member and tell them something special in person or start a Snapchat streak with them (1 HP)	Put your phone away or switch the TV off for 1 family dinner and have a conversation starting with 'How was your day?' (1HP)	Go for a walk with your family. Take a family selfie (2 HP)	Go for a 30-minute walk and try not to look at your phone but be aware of the winter season and the five senses (3 HP)	Bake something seasonal or Christmas themed with family or friend such as a gingerbread man and share with the family. Take a photo (3 HP)

2	Offer to wash the dishes after a family meal or stack/ unstack the dishwasher (1 HP)	Interview your family members talking about most embarrassing/ scary/happy moments (3 HP)	Create a gadget basket and place your gadgets in there after an agreed time in the house. No electronic device an hour before bed (includes Xbox, PlayStation, phones etc.) (3 HP)	Watch/ listen to the headline news; note down if it changes during the day. Reflect on what is the biggest crisis in our world today (1 HP)	Make a Christmas card for a family member. Take a photo (1 HP)
3	Before you get asked, offer to clean your bedroom (even if you share). Take a photo before and after (3 HP)	Write a thank you card to a teacher/ parent/friend who helps you a lot. Give it to them (3 HP)	Lie down and read a non-digital book/ magazine/ newspaper and *relax* for 20 minutes (2 HP)	When you wake up, think of five things you're grateful for and text or email them to yourself or write down or take a photo of what you are grateful for (2 HP)	Try to tell a new, short, clean joke to a family member or friend. Try to collect as many 'clean' jokes as you can for your tutor group and write a family or tutor group joke book (3 HP)
4	Put together a Christmas essentials food box for the local food bank (2 HP)	Play a board game with a family member – don't cheat, and congratulate the winner if you lose (3 HP)	Eat three different healthy breakfasts. Take photos of how different they were. Share the recipes (3 HP)	Download your schools recommend mental wellbeing app or a free mindfulness app (there are quite a few if you search) and practice the breathing exercises (3 HP)	Take part in an inter- house activity. Get your tutor group to cheer you on. How did that feel? (2 HP)

| 5 | As a family, put up the Christmas decorations and take four photographs of during and after *or* talk about what are meaningful free gifts you can give to each other. (4 HP) | Watch a favourite TV programme/film with a family member or friend and cook homemade pop-corn. What was the film/TV programme? (3 HP) | Drink seven glasses of water for a day. What do you notice at the end of the day? Always carry a full water bottle (2 HP) | Magic Moments – Get yourself a jar/box/envelope to write or store lovely experiences in. Include time with family and friends, celebration days, personal experiences. When you are feeling anxious, open your 'Magic Moments' and check how great you are (3 HP) | Either play an instrument, board game or sport you have not played in a while or learn to play a new one. Try and involve one family member (3 HP) |

Parents, please write a signature in each box after your child and/or family has successfully achieved each activity.

Want to have positive mental wellbeing as a family? Embrace these GREAT values. Parent activities #familyMH5aday				
Week	G = GIVE	R = RELATE	E = ENERGISE	A = AWARENESS	T = TRY SOMETHING NEW
1	Give someone else in the family a break from a chore they always/ usually do. Take over shopping/ washing etc. for a day/ weekend/the festive season	Aim to have five family meals without any gadgets/TV/ phones and have a family conversation	Go for a walk with your family/ run/cycle, exploring a new area	Go for an evening moonlit walk with some of your family. Notice the evening sky and how things are different from the day. Chat about the day	Bake/cook something you haven't tried before with a family member – Christmas or seasonal themed – and share with the family. Take a photo
2	Give yourself some *me time*. Let the family know so you are not interrupted but make sure you take 30 minutes out of the day just for you. Treat yourself	Phone or Skype an older family member who lives away from you and whom you have not spoken to for a while, and have a long conversation	Turn off the wifi at meal time, and before bedtime, or just for an hour a day	Watch/ listen to the headline news; note down if it changes during the day. Reflect on what is the biggest crisis in our world today with your family over a dinner conversation	Let your children try to teach you something. For example, getting them to teach you Minecraft/ Lego©, a computer game, a new dance, a maths equation or a historical fact

cont.

3	Find a charity event and either fundraise for it, or host a 'fun' event for it. It could be any charity which is either topical for that month or means something to you. For example, Movember or breast cancer	Give each child some one-to-one time, doing something together for a set time with no disruptions. Possibly ask them open-ended questions about their school, friends, anxieties and dreams. Have fun together	Lie down and read a non-digital book/ magazine and *relax* for 30 minutes. Take a photo of what you were reading or give yourself a home pamper session, or do both	When you wake up, think of five things you're grateful for and text or email them to yourself or write down or take a photo of what you are grateful for	Take part in a hobby or activity that another family member/ friend does
4	Let your child see you doing something for someone else, e.g. helping a neighbour or grandparent/ visiting a nursing or care home/ making cakes for someone/ showing you care for others	Watch one YouTube video from Time to Change about mental wellbeing. Discuss what it means to have positive mental wellbeing with a family member	Eat three different healthy breakfasts and introduce healthy snacks into the house for the family to eat. Drink more water	Write down what are your most stressful points in the day. Think about what you can do to de-stress the triggers. Different habits, perhaps? Different approaches? Talk to your family if you need help	Read a magazine or newspaper or non-fiction book you would not normally read. Finish it. Take a photo of your most interesting page

| 5 | Organise an alternative advent calendar where the kids are encouraged to put one thing into a box for the homeless or something for the foodbank | Play some games together with the family. Go to the cinema or let someone else in the family choose the DVD to watch | Go out on the bikes with a sketch pad and draw something en route or take photos of striking scenes | Magic Moments – Get yourself a jar or envelope to write or store lovely experiences. Include time with family and friends, celebration days, personal experiences. When you are feeling anxious, open your 'Magic Moments' and check how great you are | Go to a gig/ concert in a music genre you wouldn't say you like. Likewise, buy a novel in a style you wouldn't normally choose. If you never do, go to the ballet/rugby. Just extend yourself and *live* |

References

Web links

www.annafreud.org/what-we-do/schools-in-mind/our-work-with-schools/
  wellbeing-measurement-for-schools

www.educationsupportpartnership.org.uk/staff-engagement-wellbeing

https://mindfulnessinschools.org/teach-b-foundations

www.mentallyhealthyschools.org.uk/teaching-resources/lesson-plans-and-pshe-
  resources

www.pshe-association.org.uk/curriculum-and-resources/resources/guidance-
  preparing-teach-about-mental-health-and

www.thegrid.org.uk/learning/hwb/ewb/resources/documents/exploring_
  mental_health_14-16yr_olds.pdf

www.time-to-change.org.uk/get-involved/get-involved-schools/school-resources

Books and journals

Glazzard, J. (2018) 'How are you really doing?' *Teach Primary*, March, pp.64–65

Government Response to the Consultation on 'Transforming Children and Young People's Mental Health Provision: A Green Paper' and Next Steps (2018) London: Department for Education.

Kell, E. (2018) *How to Survive in Teaching: Without Imploding, Exploding or Walking Away*. London: Bloomsbury Education.

Mental Health First Aid for Schools and Colleges Manual, 2007–2014, Mental Health First Aid (MHFA) England CIC.

Policy paper: Reducing Teacher Workload (updated 24 July 2018) London: Department for Education.

Worsley, L. (2011) *The Resilience Doughnut: The Secret of Strong Kids*. Eastwood: Lyn Worsley Psychology Services.

Worsley, L. and Hjemdal, O. (2017) 'Scale Development and Psychometric Qualities of the Resilience Doughnut Tool: a valid, solution focused and ecological measure of resilience with Australian adolescents.' *Journal of Solution-Focused Brief Therapy*, 3.